THE SECRET HIDDEN HEALING
POWER OF HERBS & SPICES

DAL MEDICINE COOKBOOK

THE SECRET HIDDEN HEALING
POWER OF HERBS & SPICES

DAL MEDICINE COOKBOOK

Heal your body, live longer,
look younger and restore your health

Lustre Press
Roli Books

Published in India by Roli Books
M-75, Greater Kailash II Market
New Delhi-110 048, India
Ph: ++91-11-40682000
E-mail: info@rolibooks.com
Website: www.rolibooks.com

Editor: Saachi Khurana
Layout design: Bhagirath Kumar

ISBN: 978-81-938608-8-5

CONTENTS

RICE

MEATS

VEGETABLES AND FRUITS

BREADS AND CAKES

SIDES AND ACCOMPANIMENTS

INTRODUCTION

This book is a tribute to the colourful diversity of Indian methods of cooking dal. The term 'dal' means 'split lentil', derived from the Sanskrit root 'to split', and many Indian meals are incomplete without it. Dal contributes greatly to the Indian diet, as it is rich in protein and vitamins; it is a staple food of this country, eaten with relish by people of all financial backgrounds, throughout the year. In India, it is cooked with peerless culinary skill and innovation. There are myriad ways to prepare it, some of which are as a thick gruel, a more watery rasam, or even a fritter. As such, dal is often accompanied with flatbread or rice, and can also be eaten by itself.

The book contains over 70 recipes, showcasing the range of ways in which dal can be cooked, including Khatta Mag (sweet and sour green gram), Urad Kachori (fried bread with black gram), Dar Ni Pori (stuffed wheat and rice cake), and Dhansak (lamb cooked with mixed grams and vegetables). The reader will not run out of delicious things to eat. Whether looking for a quick, simple dish or an extravagant meal, this book is the ideal guide.

CURRIES, GRAVIES, AND STEWS

SERVES 2–4

NARKEL CHOLA DAL

Bengal gram with coconut

COOKING TIME
45 MINUTES

• Ingredients •

- 1 cup / 200 g Bengal gram (*chana dal*)
- 1 tsp turmeric (*haldi*) powder
- 2 Tbsp / 30 ml oil
- 1 tsp aniseed (*saunf*)
- 1 stick cinnamon (*dalchini*)
- 4 tsp coconut, fresh, thin, small pieces
- 1 tsp salt
- 2 tsp sugar

• Method •

1 Boil the Bengal gram with turmeric powder and enough water till done.

2 Heat the oil and sauté the aniseed and cinnamon. Add the coconut and sauté further for 5 minutes.

3 Add the boiled Bengal gram and then cook for 10 minutes.

4 Mix in the salt and sugar. Serve hot.

Cinnamon is a powerful healing spice and can improve blood sugar levels for people with diabetes. It reduces insulin resistance and consequently, lowers blood sugar levels.

SERVES 2–4

BHAJA MOONG DAL

Broiled green gram

COOKING TIME
40 MINUTES

• Ingredients •

- 1 cup / 200 g split green gram (*dhuli moong dal*), washed
- 2 Tbsp / 30 ml oil
- 2 tsp aniseed (*saunf*)
- 3 cloves (*laung*)
- 3 green chillies, slit
- 1 tsp sugar
- Salt to taste

• Method •

1 Broil the split green gram on a griddle (*tawa*) till golden brown.

2 Boil 2 cups water and cook the split green gram till done.

3 Heat the oil in a small pan; add aniseed, cloves and green chillies. Sauté just for a few seconds and then add to the split green gram.

4 Add the sugar and salt, stir well and serve immediately.

Cloves would provide fiber and important vitamins and minerals like vitamin K, vitamin C and manganese. The fiber in cloves can reduce constipation and certain compounds can reduce stomach ulcers.

SERVES 3–4

SURATI DAL

Red gram cooked with tomatoes and peanuts

COOKING TIME
25 MINUTES

• Ingredients •

- ½ cup / 100 g split red gram (*dhuli masoor dal*)
- 2 medium-size tomatoes, grated
- 8–10 peanuts, unroasted, skin removed
- 2 green chillies
- 1 Tbsp / 21 g jaggery (*gur*)
- 6–8 curry leaves (*kadhi patta*)
- ½ tsp turmeric (*haldi*) powder
- ½ tsp red chilli powder
- Salt to taste
- 2 tsp ghee
- 1 tsp mustard seeds (*rai*)
- A pinch asafoetida (*hing*)
- Juice of 1 lemon
- Green coriander (*hara dhaniya*) for garnishing

• Method •

1 Boil the split red gram and the tomatoes in 2½ cups water for 15 minutes or till soft. Stir constantly till a smooth consistency is obtained.

2 Add the peanuts, green chillies, jaggery, curry leaves, turmeric powder, red chilli powder, and salt. Bring the mixture to a boil.

3 Heat the ghee in a small pan and add the mustard seeds; when they splutter, add the asafoetida. Remove from the heat and add this tempering to the cooked split red gram. Bring the mixture to a boil again; mix in the lemon juice.

4 Serve hot, garnished with green coriander.

Curry leaves can treat an upset stomach and can be used to manage conditions like diarrhea, dysentery and constipation. They can eliminate the bacteria from your body and can prevent iron deficiency anemia.

SERVES 3–4

MEETHI DAL

Sweet and tangy split red gram

COOKING TIME
25 MINUTES

• Ingredients •

- 1 cup / 200 g split red gram (*dhuli masoor dal*), soaked for 1 hour
- 3 cups / 720 ml water
- 12 peanuts, unroasted, with skin removed
- 15 curry leaves (*kadhi patta*)
- 1 Tbsp / 21 g jaggery (*gur*)
- Juice of 1 lemon
- 3 pcs / 1 Tbsp / 15 g *cocum* or tamarind (*imli*) extract

For the tempering:

- 2 Tbsp / 30 g ghee
- ½ tsp mustard seeds (*rai*)
- 1 tsp cumin (*jeera*) seeds
- ½ tsp fenugreek seeds (*methi dana*)
- A pinch asafoetida (*hing*)
- ½ tsp turmeric (*haldi*) powder
- ½ tsp red chilli powder
- 1 tsp coriander-cumin (*dhaniya-jeera*) powder
- Salt to taste

• Method •

1 Pressure-cook the split red gram in 2 cups water till 3 whistles. Release the pressure and open the lid carefully. Whip until thick; mix in 1 cup water.

2 For the tempering, heat the ghee in a pan; sauté the tempering ingredients for a few seconds, and pour over the boiled red gram.

3 Add the remaining ingredients and cook covered for 10 minutes on medium heat. Serve hot.

Tamarind is widely used in South Asian cooking. It possesses considerable amounts of fiber which eases digestion. It has high quantities of many important nutrients. Its antioxidant qualities help the body develop resistance against infections.

SERVES 5–6

KHATTA MAG

Sweet and sour green gram

COOKING TIME
20 MINUTES

• Ingredients •

- 1 cup / 200 g whole green gram (*sabut moong dal*), soaked in warm water for 1 hour
- 1 cup / 240 g yoghurt
- 2 green chillies, ground
- 1 1-in. piece ginger, ground
- ½ tsp turmeric (*haldi*) powder
- 1 tsp red chilli powder
- 1 tsp cumin-coriander (*jeera-dhaniya*) powder
- ½ tsp jaggery (*gur*)
- Salt to taste

For the tempering:

- 1 Tbsp / 15 ml vegetable oil
- ½ tsp mustard seeds (*rai*)
- ½ tsp cumin (*jeera*) seeds
- ¼ tsp asafoetida (*hing*)

• Method •

1 Add 3 cups water to the whole green gram and pressure-cook for 10 minutes or until it is well cooked. Remove from the heat and whisk till it is well mixed and smooth.

2 Reheat the green gram and add yoghurt, green chillies, ginger, turmeric powder, red chilli powder, cumin-coriander powder, jaggery, and salt. Simmer for 10 minutes.

3 **For the tempering**, heat the oil in a pan; add the mustard seeds. When they start crackling, add cumin seeds and asafoetida.

4 Mix into the green gram mixture, and adjust seasoning. Simmer for 5 minutes and serve hot.

Asafoetida is an age-old medicine for stomach problems like gas, bloating, constipation and diarrhea due to its anti-spasmodic and anti-inflammatory properties.

SERVES 4

CREAMY BLACK GRAM

COOKING TIME
1 HOUR

• Ingredients •

- 1 cup / 200 g black gram (*urad dal*)
- 7½ cups / 1½ L water
- Salt to taste
- 3 Tbsp / 45 g ginger-garlic (*adrak-lasan*) paste
- ½ cup / 120 g tomato purée
- 5 tsp red chilli paste
- ½ cup / 120 g white butter
- ½ cup / 120 ml cream, plus more for garnishing
- 2 tsp green coriander (*hara dhaniya*), chopped

• Method •

1 Soak black gram in water and boil along with salt until the black gram is tender and the water has reduced to ¼ its original amount.

2 Stir in ginger-garlic paste, tomato purée, red chilli paste, white butter and cream. Mix well and cook for about 45 minutes on very low heat.

3 Adjust seasoning to taste and cook further for 5 minutes.

4 Remove from heat into a serving bowl. Sprinkle cream on top and garnish with chopped green coriander. Serve hot.

Coriander is an abundant source of dietary fiber, manganese, iron, magnesium, vitamin C and protein. Including coriander in your regular diet can lower blood pressure, lower bad cholesterol levels and improve good cholesterol levels.

SERVES 4–5

PUNJABI CHANA MASALA

COOKING TIME
1 HOUR

Bengal gram, cooked the traditional Punjabi way

• Ingredients •

- 1¼ cups / 250 g whole Bengal gram (*chana dal*)
- 7½ cups / 1½ L water
- 1 bay leaf (*tej patta*)
- 1 stick cinnamon (*dalchini*)
- 2⅔ Tbsp / 40 g butter
- ½ cup / 85 g onions, chopped
- 1⅓ tsp garam masala
- 2 tsp ginger paste
- 2 tsp garlic paste
- 4 Tbsp / 60 g tomatoes, skinned, chopped
- Salt to taste
- 1 tsp green coriander (*hara dhaniya*), chopped

• Method •

1 Clean the Bengal gram, wash in water 3 or 4 times and soak for 30 minutes.

2 Boil water in a saucepan. Add the bay leaf, cinnamon stick and the drained Bengal gram; bring to a slow boil. Remove the scum from the top of the pan and simmer until the gram is completely cooked and tender. Discard the bay leaf and cinnamon sticks.

3 Heat the butter in a pan and sauté the onions till they are soft and golden. Add the garam masala and ginger and garlic pastes and sauté over medium heat for 2–3 minutes.

4 Add the tomatoes, cooked gram and salt. Cover and cook for another 2–3 minutes. Serve hot, garnished with green coriander.

Bay leaves aid in digestion by boosting appetite, reducing flatulence and helping with gastric diseases.

DAL SULTANI

SERVES 4–5

Red gram seasoned with saffron

COOKING TIME
30 MINUTES

• Ingredients •

- 1¼ cups / 250 g red gram (*masoor dal*)
- 1 tsp turmeric (*haldi*) powder
- Salt to taste
- ¼ cup / 60 g butter
- ¾ cup / 150 g onions, quartered
- 1 tsp black cumin (*shahi jeera*) seeds
- 2 tsp red chilli powder
- 2 Tbsp / 30 ml cream
- A pinch saffron, soaked in cream

• Method •

1 Wash the gram 3 or 4 times in running water and soak for 30 minutes in cold water.

2 In a heavy pan, boil 2 L water. Add the red gram and return to boil. Remove the scum from the top.

3 Reduce the heat. Add ⅔ of the turmeric powder. Cover and cook until the gram is completely soft. Add salt.

4 In a separate pan, heat butter on low heat. Add onions and sauté over medium heat. Add the black cumin seeds, the remaining turmeric powder and red chilli powder and stir. When the seeds begin to splutter, add the cooked gram. Cover and cook for 2–3 minutes.

5 Pour the cream-saffron mixture over the cooked gram and serve with boiled rice.

Saffron is rich in antioxidants. Tremendously beneficial for the nervous system, it protects brain cells against progressive damage.

PARUPPU PAYASAM

SERVES 4

Green gram and jaggery in coconut milk

COOKING TIME
40 MINUTES

• Ingredients •

- ½ cup / 100 g green gram (*moong dal*)
- 2 Tbsp / 30 g ghee
- 2 Tbsp / 30 g cashew nuts (*kaju*), broken
- 2 cups / 480 ml coconut milk, first and last extracts separated
- 1 cup / 240 g jaggery (*gur*), powdered
- 3 green cardamoms (*choti elaichi*), crushed

• Method •

1 Fry the cashew nuts in 1 Tbsp ghee. Keep aside.

2 Dry-roast the green gram in a pan for a few minutes or till it turns golden. Add some water and cook until the gram starts to soften.

3 Add the last two extracts of coconut milk and simmer on low heat till the gram is fully cooked.

4 Add the first extract of coconut milk, jaggery and green cardamom powder; simmer for another minute till it blends well.

5 Remove from heat and add the cashew nuts. Top with the remaining ghee and serve hot.

Cardamoms have a diuretic effect. They remove excess water from the body. They are rich in compounds that fight inflammation and can protect the body from chronic diseases.

SERVES 6–7

KATHI DAL

Tangy split green gram

COOKING TIME
20 MINUTES

• Ingredients •

- 1 cup / 200 g split green gram (*dhuli moong dal*), soaked for 30 minutes, drained
- 2 Tbsp / 30 g ghee
- ½ tsp cumin (*jeera*) seeds
- A pinch asafoetida (*hing*)
- ½ tsp turmeric (*haldi*) powder
- Salt to taste
- 3 cups / 720 ml water

• Method •

1 Heat the ghee in a pressure cooker; add the cumin seeds and asafoetida. When the seeds start spluttering, add the split green gram. Sauté for 2 minutes.

2 Add turmeric powder, salt and 3 cups water. Mix well and close the pressure cooker. Cook till 3 whistles. Remove from heat and allow the pressure to release slowly.

3 Mix the green gram mixture with a ladle and serve hot with steamed rice.

Traditionally, **cumin seeds** are used to aid digestion as they have been noted to increase the activity of digestive enzymes. They have also shown to promote weight loss, boost your immune system, promote detoxification.

KEERAI MASIYAL

SERVES 4

Mashed amaranth with green gram

COOKING TIME
15 MINUTES

• Ingredients •

- 2 bunches amaranth leaves, washed, finely chopped
- ¾ cup / 150 g green gram (*moong dal*)
- Salt to taste

For the tempering:

- 1 Tbsp / 15 ml refined oil
- ½ tsp mustard seeds (*rai*)
- 1 tsp black gram (*urad dal*)
- 1 dried red chilli (*sookhi lal mirch*)
- 1 tsp cumin (*jeera*) seeds
- ¼ tsp asafoetida (*hing*)

• Method •

1 Boil the green gram in 1½ cups water and cook till soft (2 whistles); keep aside.

2 Boil about ½ cup water with salt. Add the amaranth leaves and cook till they turn soft. Remove and mash lightly.

3 Add the boiled green gram and mix well.

4 **For the tempering**, heat the oil in a pan; sauté the mustard seeds till they start crackling. Add the remaining ingredients and sauté till the black gram turns golden.

5 Add the amaranth mixture and mix well.

6 Serve hot.

Amaranth leaves contain high levels of calcium that support bone strength and can prevent osteoporosis. Regularly consuming these leaves can help maintain the balance of electrolytes in the body and can prevent macular degeneration.

SERVES 2–4

KHATTI TUR DAL

Tangy red gram

COOKING TIME
40 MINUTES

• Ingredients •

- 1 cup / 200 g split red gram (*dhuli masoor dal*)
- 3 cups / 720 ml water
- ½ tsp turmeric (*haldi*) powder
- Salt to taste
- 2 Tbsp / 30 g ghee
- 1 grain asafoetida (*hing*)
- 1 tsp sugar / jaggery (*gur*)
- 2 medium-size tomatoes, blanched, seeds removed
- Juice of 1 lemon
- A bunch green coriander (*hara dhaniya*), chopped

For the paste:

- 1 1-in. piece ginger
- 5 garlic cloves
- 8 black peppercorns (*sabut kali mirch*)
- 1 1-in. stick cinnamon (*dalchini*)
- 1 tsp coriander (*dhaniya*) seeds
- 1 tsp cumin (*jeera*) seeds
- 4 green chillies, slit

• Method •

1 Boil the split red gram in water with turmeric powder and salt for 25 minutes or till a thick soup-like consistency is obtained.

2 Grind the ingredients mentioned to a fine paste.

3 Heat the ghee in a pan; add the asafoetida, sugar / jaggery, and tomatoes; sauté for 2 minutes. Add the paste and stir-fry for 5 minutes on low heat.

4 Add the red gram and cook till thick. Mix in the lemon juice. Serve garnished with green coriander.

Black peppercorns come from vines and are dried to use as a spice. When added to your food, they can stimulate digestive juices and enzymes, improving the body's ability to break down and digest food.

SERVES 2–4

LOBIA TARIWALA

Black-eyed peas curry

COOKING TIME
45 MINUTES

• Ingredients •

- 1 cup / 200 g black-eyed peas (*lobia*)
- 1 tsp turmeric (*haldi*) powder
- Salt to taste
- ¼ tsp asafoetida (*hing*)
- ½ cup / 120 g ghee
- ½ cup / 85 g onions, chopped
- 2 tsp garlic, chopped
- 2 tsp ginger, chopped
- 3 red chillies, whole
- ½ cup / 120 g tomatoes, chopped
- 1 tsp coriander seeds (*dhaniya*)
- 2 tsp red chilli powder
- 2 tsp cumin (*jeera*) powder
- 2 tsp coriander (*dhaniya*) powder
- 1 tsp garam masala

• Method •

1 Boil the black-eyed peas in a pressure cooker with turmeric powder, salt, asafoetida and 3 cups water for 15–20 minutes.

2 Heat the ghee in a wok (*kadhai*); add the onions, garlic, ginger and whole red chillies. Sauté till onions are light brown.

3 Add the tomatoes, coriander seeds, red chilli powder, cumin powder, coriander powder and garam masala. Fry till the tomatoes turn soft.

4 Pour in the boiled black-eyed peas mixture with the water. Mix well.

5 Serve hot.

Garlic can lower heart disease risk and reduces cholesterol levels. Garlic is a heart-healthy seasoning which can act as a natural blood thinner, which can prevent dangerous clots. Its compounds flush out carcinogens and helps with circulation.

SERVES 4–6

DHAN DAR

Split red gram tempered with garlic

COOKING TIME
20 MINUTES

• Ingredients •

- ½ cup / 100 g split red gram (*dhuli masoor dal*)
- ¼ tsp salt
- ¼ tsp turmeric (*haldi*) powder
- Fried onions for garnishing
- Butter for garnishing

For the tempering:

- 2 Tbsp / 30 ml vegetable oil
- 2 green chillies
- A pinch salt
- ¼ tsp garlic paste or 4–5 garlic cloves, chopped
- ¼ tsp cumin (*jeera*) seeds or powder

• Method •

1 Soak the split red gram in 2–3 cups water with salt and turmeric powder for at least 20 minutes. Most of the water should be absorbed.

2 Transfer the split red gram into a pressure cooker. Add water, about ½ in. above the gram level. Cook on high heat. After the first whistle, turn heat to low and cook for 5 minutes. Keep aside to cool.

3 Whisk or blend, adding water, if required. Return the cooker to heat and bring it to a boil.

4 **For the tempering**, heat the oil in a pan till it smokes; lower heat, sauté all the ingredients till golden. Remove from heat, pour into the gram, and cover immediately to prevent the aroma from escaping.

5 Simmer for 2–3 minutes before serving, garnished with fried onions and a dollop of butter.

Turmeric gives a fierce yellow colour and stimulates the natural detox function in the body. It is beneficial for people with high blood pressure and can lower hypertension.

SERVES 2–4

DAL MOONG-MASOOR

Two-in-one dal

COOKING TIME
45 MINUTES

• Ingredients •

- ½ cup / 100 g green gram (*moong dal*)
- ½ cup / 100 g red gram (*masoor dal*)
- 1 tsp turmeric (*haldi*) powder
- Salt to taste
- ½ cup / 120 g ghee
- ½ cup / 85 g onions, chopped
- 2 tsp garlic, chopped
- 1 tsp cumin (*jeera*) seeds
- ½ cup / 120 g tomatoes, chopped
- 2 tsp coriander (*dhaniya*) powder
- 1 tsp red chilli powder
- ½ cup / 8 g green coriander (*hara dhaniya*), chopped

• Method •

1 Boil the green and red gram in 2 cups water with turmeric powder and salt. Cook until tender. Keep aside.

2 Heat the ghee in a wok (*kadhai*); add the onions, garlic and cumin seeds. Fry till light brown.

3 Add the tomatoes, coriander powder and red chilli powder and sauté till the tomatoes turn soft. Add this to the cooked gram mixture. Mix well.

4 Serve hot, garnished with green coriander.

Dried, chopped or powdered, adding small amounts of these chillies to your food can provide your body with vitamin A and C, copper, and potassium. They also have high quantities of antioxidant carotenoids, which have numerous health benefits.

SERVES 4–6

AMRITSARI DAL

Split black gram flavoured with mint

COOKING TIME
45 MINUTES

• Ingredients •

- 1 cup / 200 g split black gram (*dhuli urad dal*), soaked for 1 hour
- ½ cup / 100 g Bengal gram (*chana dal*), soaked for 1 hour
- Salt to taste
- 2 Tbsp / 30 g ginger, chopped
- 2 Tbsp / 30 g garlic, chopped
- ½ cup / 120 g unsalted butter
- ½ cup / 120 g ghee
- ½ cup / 85 g onions, chopped
- 6 green chillies, chopped
- ¼ cup / 60 g tomatoes, chopped
- 1 Tbsp / 4 g mint leaves

• Method •

1 Drain both the grams and cook in 5 cups water in a large pan; add salt. Bring to a boil, reduce the heat and keep removing the scum that surfaces.

2 Add 1½ Tbsp of ginger and garlic each and unsalted butter. Cook covered until the mixed gram is tender and a little water remains. Remove and mash the mixture against the sides of the pan with a large spoon.

3 Heat the ghee in a pan; add the onions and fry until light brown. Add the remaining ginger and garlic, green chillies, tomatoes and mint leaves. Cook until the tomatoes are pulpy. Pour this into the above mixture and stir. Serve hot.

Due to its benefits to oral care, **mint** can often be spotted in chewing gums and breath fresheners. Mint can work wonders for your digestive system. It aids digestion and can soothe an upset stomach.

SERVES 4–6

SEYAL CHANRAN JI DAL

Bengal gram with spices

COOKING TIME
25 MINUTES

• Ingredients •

- ¾ cup / 150 g Bengal gram (*chana dal*), soaked for 10 minutes, drained
- 2 Tbsp / 30 ml vegetable oil
- 2 medium-size onions, finely chopped
- 1 tsp coriander (*dhaniya*) powder
- 1 tsp red chilli powder
- 2 cups / 480 ml water
- 2 medium-size tomatoes, finely chopped
- 1 Tbsp / 15 g ginger, cut into slivers
- 4 green chillies, slit
- Salt to taste
- ½ tsp garam masala
- 4 Tbsp / 4 g green coriander (*hara dhaniya*) for garnishing

• Method •

1 Heat the oil in a pressure cooker; fry the onions till light brown. Add gram, coriander powder, and red chilli powder; fry for a few minutes. Add 1½ cups water and cook till 2 whistles or 10 minutes.

2 After the steam comes out, open the lid. Add tomatoes, ginger, green chillies, and salt; stir-fry till the tomatoes are cooked.

3 Add ½ cup water and garam masala. Cook till 1 whistle on high heat.

4 Serve hot, garnished with green coriander.

Garam Masala is a fragrant blend of many Indian spices. Using it in your recipes means that you can harness the flavours and health benefits of many spices and herbs to improve your blood sugar and lower cholesterol levels.

SERVES 6-8

DAL MAKHNI

Easy-to-make split green gram

COOKING TIME
10 MINUTES

• Ingredients •

- 1 cup / 200 g split green gram (*dhuli moong dal*), washed, soaked
- ½ tsp turmeric (*haldi*) powder
- 2 cups / 480 ml water
- ½ tsp salt
- ½ tsp black pepper
- ½ tsp raw mango powder (*amchoor*)
- 2 Tbsp / 30 g ghee

• Method •

1 Pressure-cook the gram with turmeric powder and 2 cups water till 2 whistles.

2 After the steam comes out, open the lid. Add salt and mash the gram.

3 Transfer the gram to a serving bowl. Sprinkle with black pepper and mango powder.

4 Heat the ghee in a small pan and pour over the gram.

5 Serve hot with puris, if desired.

Very popular in Indian cuisine, **raw mango powder** offers high nutritional value as it includes nutrients like vitamin A, E and C, along with antioxidants. It can improve digestion and reduce acidity. Aamchoor helps in detoxifying your body.

SERVES 6–8

TI DALI

Three-in-one lentil

COOKING TIME
25 MINUTES

• Ingredients •

- ½ cup / 100 g split red gram (*dhuli masoor dal*)
- ½ cup / 100 g split Bengal gram (*chana dal*)
- ½ cup / 100 g split green gram (*dhuli moong dal*)
- ½ tsp turmeric (*haldi*) powder
- ½ cup / 120 g medium-size tomatoes, cut into fine pieces
- 1 tsp ginger, finely chopped
- 2 green chillies, chopped
- Salt to taste
- 2 Tbsp / 30 ml vegetable oil
- 6 garlic cloves
- 1 tsp red chilli powder

• Method •

1 Put all the grams together in a pressure cooker along with turmeric powder and 2 cups water. Cook till 3 whistles on simmer. When the steam comes out, add tomatoes, ginger, green chillies, and salt. Stir well and cook without covering, till the tomatoes are cooked.

2 Heat the oil in a pan; fry garlic till brownish. Remove the pan from the heat and add red chilli powder. Pour this garlic mixture into the gram and mix well.

3 Serve hot, garnished with green coriander and accompanied with rotis, if desired.

Green chillies are used in many forms in Indian cuisine. A rich source of vitamin C, they can keep your skin healthy.

SERVES 3

ELUMICHAPAZHAM RASAM

Thin green gram soup with lemon

COOKING TIME
20 MINUTES

• Ingredients •

- Juice of 2 lemons
- 1½ Tbsp / 30 g green gram (*moong dal*)

For the tempering:
- 1 Tbsp / 15 ml refined oil
- ¼ tsp mustard seeds (*rai*)
- 1 1-in. piece ginger, finely chopped
- 1 green chilli, slit
- 1½ cups / 360 ml water
- ½ tsp turmeric (*haldi*) powder
- A small bunch green coriander (*hara dhaniya*), finely chopped

• Method •

1 Boil the green gram in enough water to cover till soft. Remove, mash and keep aside.

2 For the tempering, heat the oil in a pan; sauté the mustard seeds till they start crackling. Add ginger and green chilli; sauté for a while.

3 Mix the green gram with the tempering, add water and turmeric powder. Bring the mixture to a boil on low heat.

4 Add lemon juice; mix well.

5 Serve hot, garnished with green coriander.

Ginger is primarily used as a digestive aid. It is good for your digestive track and very effective against nausea.

SERVES 4

ARAITHUVUTTU RASAM

COOKING TIME
15 MINUTES

Soup made with ground spices

• Ingredients •

- 1 medium-size tomato, diced
- 2 Tbsp / 30 ml refined oil
- 1 Tbsp / 5 g coriander (*dhaniya*) seeds
- 2 Tbsp / 25 g Bengal gram (*chana dal*)
- 1 dried red chilli (*sookhi lal mirch*)
- 1 tsp black pepper
- 1 Tbsp / 4 g coconut, grated
- 1 lemon-size tamarind (*imli*)
- ½ tsp mustard seeds (*rai*)
- A few curry leaves (*kadhi patta*)

• Method •

1 Heat ½ Tbsp oil in a pan; sauté the coriander seeds, Bengal gram, dried red chilli, and black pepper until the gram turns golden. Add coconut and stir for a few minutes.

2 Remove from heat and grind to make a coarse paste, sprinkling a little water if necessary.

3 Bring the tamarind, tomato, and the paste to a boil in a pot.

4 Heat the remaining oil in a pan; add mustard seeds and curry leaves. When the seeds start crackling, remove and add to the tomato mixture.

5 Serve hot as a soup or with steamed rice.

Curry leaves work against obesity and regulate cholesterol levels in the body. They support the health of your heart and improve your memory.

CHANE KI DAL

SERVES 2–4

Bengal gram flavoured with tomatoes

COOKING TIME
45 MINUTES

• Ingredients •

- 1 cup / 200 g split Bengal gram (*chana dal*)
- ½ cup / 100 g split black gram (*dhuli urad dal*)
- 3 black cardamoms (*badi elaichi*)
- 1 tsp turmeric (*haldi*) powder
- ¼ tsp asafoetida (*hing*)
- Salt to taste
- ½ cup / 120 g ghee
- ½ cup / 85 g onions, chopped
- 2 tsp garlic, chopped
- 1 cup / 240 g tomatoes, chopped
- 2 tsp red chilli powder
- 2 tsp coriander (*dhaniya*) powder
- 3 tsp ginger, chopped
- 1 tsp cumin (*jeera*) powder
- 1 tsp garam masala
- 5 green chillies, chopped
- ½ cup / 8 g green coriander (*hara dhaniya*), chopped

• Method •

1 Boil the split Bengal gram and black gram in 3 cups water with black cardamoms, turmeric powder, asafoetida and salt. Cook till tender. Keep aside.

2 Heat the ghee in a wok (*kadhai*); add the onions and garlic and fry till light brown.

3 Add the remaining ingredients, except green coriander. Cook till the tomatoes turn soft. Add this to the split Bengal gram mixture. Mix well.

4 Serve hot, garnished with green coriander.

Cardamoms can improve your respiratory health, especially is someone is suffering from asthma, lung congestion, and bronchitis. The strong aroma can cure halitosis and prevent dental disorders like teeth and gum infections.

SERVES 6–8

THUHAR JI DAL

Tangy red gram

COOKING TIME
30 MINUTES

• Ingredients •

- 1 cup / 200 gm split red gram (*arhar dal*), washed
- 3 cups / 750 ml water
- ½ tsp turmeric (*haldi*) powder
- 2 tbsp vegetable oil
- 1 tsp cumin (*jeera*) seeds
- a pinch asafoetida (*hing*)
- 1 tbsp / 10 gm chickpea flour (*besan*)
- 3 tomatoes, pulp only
- 1 tamarind (*imli*), walnut-sized, soaked
- Salt to taste
- 1 tsp red chilli powder
- 1 tbsp green chillies, slit for garnishing
- Green coriander (*hara dhaniya*) for garnishing

• Method •

1 Boil the dal in a pressure cooker with 2 cups water and turmeric powder till at least 2 whistles or 10 minutes.

2 Heat the oil in a separate wok (*kadhai*); add cumin seeds. When the seeds begin to crackle, add asafoetida and chickpea flour; sauté the flour till brown. Add 1 cup water and cook for a few minutes.

3 Add tomato pulp, tamarind pulp, and salt.

4 Mix this sauce with the dal and cook again for a few minutes.

5 Serve hot garnished with slit green chillies and green coriander and accompanied with rice.

SERVES 3–4

PATLI MANGORI

Green gram pieces in tomato gravy

COOKING TIME
20 MINUTES

• Ingredients •

- 1 cup / 200 g *mangori*, coarsely crushed
- 2 Tbsp / 30 g ghee
- A pinch asafoetida (*hing*)
- ½ tsp cumin (*jeera*) seeds
- 1 1-in. piece ginger, finely chopped
- 1 green chilli, slit
- Salt to taste ¼ tsp turmeric (*haldi*) powder
- 1½ cups / 360 ml water
- 1 large tomato, chopped
- 1 tsp red chilli powder
- ½ tsp mango powder (*amchoor*)
- 4 Tbsp / 4 g green coriander (*hara dhaniya*), chopped

For the mangori:

- 1¼ cups / 250 g split green gram (*dhuli moong dal*), soaked for 2 hours
- A pinch asafoetida (*hing*)

• Method •

1 For the *mangori*, drain and grind the split green gram to a smooth and thick consistency. Add the asafoetida and whip together for 2–3 minutes. Grease a 4 ft x 2 ft plastic sheet lightly on one side. Put some green gram paste in a ½ kg-size polythene packet and make a small hole in one corner of the packet.

2 Now squeeze the paste out gradually onto the greased sheet in long thin strands and sun-dry. Repeat till all the paste is used up. When it has completely dried, the *mangori* will come off on its own. Store in airtight jars.

3 Heat the ghee in a wok (*kadhai*); add the asafoetida, cumin seeds, ginger, and green chilli. Add the *mangori* and sauté for 2 minutes. Add salt, turmeric powder, and water. Bring the mixture to a boil, lower heat and simmer till the *mangori* is tender.

4 Increase the heat and add the remaining ingredients, except green coriander. Boil till the gravy is smooth and thick.

5 Serve hot, garnished with green coriander.

Turmeric is known for its warm nature and bitter flavour, it has qualities that boost the body's antioxidant enzymes. It has anti-inflammatory health benefits and can be used for a variety of conditions from menstrual difficulties to chronic diseases.

SERVES 6–8

PANCHMELA DAL

Five-in-one pulse delight

COOKING TIME
1 HOUR

• Ingredients •

- 2½ Tbsp / 30 g split green gram (*dhuli moong dal*)
- 3 Tbsp / 40 g whole green gram (*sabut moong dal*)
- 3 Tbsp / 40 g Bengal gram (*chana dal*)
- 2½ Tbsp / 30 g split red gram (*dhuli masoor dal*)
- 2½ Tbsp / 30 g black gram (*urad dal*)
- 2½ Tbsp / 30 g dried pea (*matar dal*)
- 4 Tbsp / 60 g ghee
- A big pinch asafoetida (*hing*)
- 1½ tsp cumin (*jeera*) seeds
- 1½-in. piece ginger, julienned
- 2–3 bay leaves (*tej patta*)
- 1 tsp coriander (*dhaniya*) powder
- 1 tsp mango powder (*amchoor*)
- 1 large tomato, chopped
- 3 cups / 720 ml water
- Salt to taste
- 1 tsp turmeric (*haldi*) powder
- 1 tsp red chilli powder
- A pinch sugar
- 1 cup plus 4 Tbsp / 20 g green coriander (*hara dhaniya*), chopped
- 1 green chilli, slit

• Method •

1 Soak all the pulses together for 30 minutes. Drain and keep aside.

2 Heat 2 Tbsp ghee in a pressure cooker; add asafoetida, cumin seeds, ginger, and bay leaves; sauté. Add the pulses and stir-fry for 2–3 minutes.

3 Add coriander powder, mango powder, and tomato; sauté again for 2–3 minutes.

4 Add water, salt, and turmeric powder and pressure-cook till 3 whistles; then allow the pressure to release by itself.

5 Heat 2 Tbsp ghee in a small pan; add the red chilli powder mixed with 3 Tbsp water and sugar. Lower heat and simmer for 1 minute to get a rich red colour.

6 Add this mixture, green coriander and green chilli to the cooked pulses. Mix well and serve hot.

Asafoeida has anti-inflammatory properties that reduce inflammation of blood vessels in the body, which can reduce headaches. Asafoetida also helps in relieving respiratory disorders like asthma and bronchitis due to anti-viral and antibiotic properties.

SERVES 4–5

CHANA PINDI

Chickpea curry

COOKING TIME
1 HOUR

• Ingredients •

- 1¼ cups / 250 g whole chickpeas (*kabuli chana*)
- 1–1⅓ tsp bicarbonate of soda
- 1 bay leaf (*tej patta*)
- 3 green / black cardamoms (*choti / badi elaichi*)
- 1 tsp chana masala
- 3 sticks cinnamon (*dalchini*)
- 1 tsp coriander (*dhaniya*) powder
- 1 tsp garam masala
- 2 tsp garlic paste
- 2 tsp ginger paste
- 1 Tbsp / 15 ml lemon juice
- 4 Tbsp / 60 ml oil
- ¾ tsp red chilli powder
- Salt for seasoning
- 1 tea bag

For garnishing:

- 10 green chillies, whole
- 3 lemons, cut into wedges
- ½ cup / 100 g onion rings
- 4 Tbsp / 60 g medium-size tomatoes, quartered

• Method •

1 Clean, wash and soak the chickpeas in water for 3 hours.

2 In a heavy pot, boil 2 L water; add the bay leaf, cinnamon sticks, cardamoms, tea bag and chickpeas. Bring back to boil and add bicarbonate of soda. Cover and cook over low heat until the chickpeas are soft. Drain immediately. Remove the bay leaf, tea bag, cinnamon sticks and cardamoms.

3 Heat the oil in a pan over low heat. Add the ginger and garlic pastes and sauté for 30–40 seconds. Add the red chilli powder, garam masala, coriander powder, chana masala, salt and lemon juice.

4 Add the cooked chickpeas, mixing carefully.

5 Garnish with the onion rings, whole green chillies, tomatoes and lemon
wedges. Serve with any Indian bread of choice.

Used in cuisines all over the world and readily available, **cinnamon** is a heart-smart spice and has the ability to reduce cholesterol and triglycerides. It is shown to have a natural ability to fight fungal and bacterial infections.

RICE

SERVES 5–6

MAG NA DAL NA KHICHRI

COOKING TIME
15 MINUTES

Green gram cooked with rice

• Ingredients •

- ¾ cup / 150 g whole green gram (*sabut moong dal*), washed, soaked for 30 minutes, drained
- ¾ cup / 150 g rice, washed, soaked for 30 minutes, drained
- 4 cups / 960 ml water, hot
- ¼ tsp turmeric (*haldi*) powder
- Salt to taste
- 6 black peppercorns (*sabut kali mirch*)
- 1 Tbsp / 15 g ghee

• Method •

1 Cook the green gram and rice in a pressure cooker. Add the water, turmeric powder, salt, and black peppercorns.

2 Allow 1 whistle, wait for the pressure in the cooker to subside and then open the cooker carefully. Add ghee, adjust seasoning and serve. It should be of pouring consistency.

Black peppercorns are a notable source of magnesium, iron, fiber and vitamin K. They have anti-cancer properties and can increase the body's protection against cancer.

SERVES 4–5

KANIKA BHOG

Aromatic green gram and rice preparation with raisins

COOKING TIME
20 MINUTES

• Ingredients •

- ¾ cup / 150 g rice, soaked for 1 hour, drained
- ¼ cup / 50 g split green gram (*dhuli moong dal*), soaked for 1 hour, drained
- 2 Tbsp / 30 g ghee
- 2 black cardamoms (*badi elaichi*)
- 4 cloves (*laung*)
- 1 tsp salt
- 3 tsp sugar
- 10–12 raisins (*kishmish*)
- 2 cups / 480 ml water

• Method •

1 Heat the ghee in a pressure pan; add the black cardamoms and cloves; sauté for a while.

2 Add the remaining ingredients; mix well. Close the pan and cook till 2 whistles. Remove the pan from the heat.

3 After 2–3 minutes, release the pressure; mix gently and serve hot.

Black cardamoms are used for their powerful flavour. They have a positive impact on your gastro-intestinal health. By regulating the amount of juices secreted in the stomach and intestines, they can heal chronic constipation and improve appetite.

SERVES 4–6

DAL KI KHICHRI

Mixed dals cooked with rice

COOKING TIME
40 MINUTES

• Ingredients •

- ½ cup / 100 g split green gram (*dhuli moong dal*)
- ½ cup / 100 g split black gram (*dhuli urad dal*)
- ½ cup / 100 g red gram (*masoor dal*)
- 1 tsp ghee
- 5 cups / 1 L water
- 3 tsp salt
- ½ tsp turmeric (*haldi*) powder
- 1 Tbsp / 15 g ginger-garlic (*adrak-lasan*) paste
- 4 cups / 800 g rice, cleaned

• Method •

1 Heat the ghee in a wok (*kadhai*); add the grams and gently fry for 5–10 minutes.

2 Add 1½ cups water and cook till all the water is absorbed and the grams are soft. Add the salt, turmeric powder, ginger-garlic paste and rice. Mix well.

3 Add the remaining water and cook on low heat until all the water is absorbed and the rice is done.

4 Serve hot.

Along with giving a little extra flavour to the dish, the **ginger-garlic paste** has anti-inflammatory, anti-fungal and antimicrobial properties. It boosts the immune system and increases chance of recovery from infections.

CHURHI KHICHRI

SERVES 4–6

Rice and green gram cooked dry

COOKING TIME
25 MINUTES

• Ingredients •

- 1½ cups / 300 g basmati rice
- ½ cup / 100 g split green gram (*dhuli moong dal*)
- 3½ cups / 840 ml water
- Salt to taste
- 2 Tbsp / 30 g ghee

• Method •

1 Mix rice and gram together. Wash and soak for 30 minutes.

2 Put soaked rice and gram in a non-stick pan. Add salt and pour water; mix well. Cook on high heat till the mixture comes to a boil.

3 Lower heat and cook covered till the mixture is dry. Stir a couple of times so that it does not stick to the bottom of the pan.

4 Heat the ghee in a small pan till smoking. Pour over the prepared rice mixture and mix thoroughly.

5 Serve hot with *sai bhaji* (see p. 60).

SERVES 4

LEMON RICE

COOKING TIME
25-35 MINUTES

• Ingredients •

- ½ cup/ 100 gm Basmati rice or any long-grain variety
- ½ tbsp / 7 gm black gram, split (*dhuli urad dal*)
- 2-2⅔ cups / 400-480 ml water
- 1 tsp / 5 gm salt
- 3 tbsp / 45 ml oil / clarified butter (*ghee*)
- ½ cup / 75 gm cashew nuts (*kaju*), chopped
- 1 tsp / 5 gm mustard (*rai*) seeds
- 2-3 red chillies, whole
- ½ tsp / 3 gm turmeric (*haldi*) powder
- ⅓ cup / 80 ml lemon juice
- 3 tbsp / 45 gm green coriander (*hara dhaniya*), coarsely chopped
- 5 tsp / 25 gm coconut (*nariyal*), fresh, shredded

• Method •

1 Wash and soak the rice in water for 10 minutes. Drain and keep aside.

2 Boil water in a heavy-bottomed pan. Stir in rice, salt and 7 ml / ½ tbsp oil. Cover tightly, reduce heat and simmer without stirring until the rice is fluffy and tender and the water is fully absorbed. Keep aside.

3 Heat remaining oil in a small pan. Stir-fry the cashew nuts until golden brown. Spoon cashew nuts over the cooked rice and replace cover.

4 Raise the heat slightly. Sauté the split black gram and mustard seeds. Add the red chillies and remove from heat.

5 Gently fold in the sautéed mixture along with turmeric powder, lemon juice, coriander and coconut into the cooked rice until well mixed.

6 Serve hot, with plain yoghurt (dahi).

SERVES 4

BISI BELE HULIYANA

Spiced sambhar with rice

COOKING TIME
40 MINUTES

• Ingredients •

- 1¼ cups / 250 g basmati rice
- ⅔ cup / 133 g red gram (*masoor dal*)
- ¼ cup / 50 g split Bengal gram (*chana dal*), husked
- 2 Tbsp / 25 g split black gram (*dhuli urad dal*), husked
- 2 1-in. sticks cinnamon (*dalchini*)
- 5 green cardamoms (*choti elaichi*)
- 5 cloves (*laung*)
- 1 tsp cumin (*jeera*) seeds
- 1 tsp fenugreek seeds (*methi dana*)
- Groundnut oil (*moongphali ka tel*) to deep-fry
- 4 tsp cashew nuts (*kaju*), split
- ¼ cup / 40 g green peas
- ½ cup / 50 g cauliflower, small florets
- 1⅔ cups / 400 g medium-size tomatoes, chopped
- 3 Tbsp / 45 g tamarind (*imli*) extract
- ½ tsp asafoetida (*hing*)
- ½ tsp red chilli powder
- 1 tsp turmeric (*haldi*) powder
- Salt to taste
- 10 curry leaves (*kadhi patta*)
- 2 Tbsp / 30 ml groundnut oil (*moongphali ka tel*) for tempering
- ½ tsp mustard seeds (*rai*)
- 2 red chillies, whole

• Method •

1 Wash rice and red gram and soak separately for 30 minutes.

2 **For the sambhar powder**, broil Bengal gram and black gram separately on a griddle till light brown.

3 Broil cinnamon, cardamoms, cloves, cumin seeds and fenugreek seeds for 30 seconds. Grind together with the broiled Bengal gram and black gram in a blender.

4 Deep-fry the cashew nuts till golden brown. Keep aside.

5 Put red gram in a pot, add 10 cups water and bring to a boil. Simmer until almost cooked.

6 Drain rice and add to the cooked gram, along with peas and cauliflower. Simmer for 10 minutes, stirring occasionally.

7 Stir in the tomatoes, tamarind extract and the asafoetida.

8 Add red chilli powder, turmeric and salt. Stir in the blended sambhar powder.

9 Cover and simmer till rice and vegetables are cooked and become porridge-like. Sprinkle curry leaves and simmer.

10 Heat 2 Tbsp groundnut oil in a wok (*kadhai*) and sauté the mustard seeds. Add whole red chillies and stir for 15 seconds.

11 Pour the tempering over the red gram-rice-vegetable mixture. Stir for 2 minutes. Garnish with cashew nuts and serve with pickle and pappadams.

Belonging to the pea family, **fenugreek seeds** can improve glycemic control, boost exercise performance, reduce inflammation, and aid digestion. They are rich in antioxidants and fiber, and can flush out harmful toxins from the body.

MEATS

SERVES 6–8

DAL GOSHT

Lamb cooked with Bengal gram

COOKING TIME
1 HOUR

• Ingredients •

- 2 lb, 3 oz / 1 kg lamb, cut into ½-in. cubes
- 1½ cups / 300 g Bengal gram (*chana dal*), soaked for 2 hours
- 6 Tbsp / 90 ml oil
- 4 tsp ginger-garlic (*adrak-lasan*) paste
- 1 tsp turmeric (*haldi*) powder
- 2 tsp red chilli powder
- 2 tsp garam masala
- 3 medium-size onions, chopped, ground into a paste
- 4 medium-size tomatoes, chopped, ground into a paste
- Salt to taste
- 1 tsp sugar
- 1 cup / 240 g yoghurt
- 5 Tbsp / 5 g green coriander (*hara dhaniya*), finely chopped

• Method •

1 Drain and cook the Bengal gram in 1 cup water till tender, but not overcooked. Drain and keep aside.

2 Heat the oil in a wok (*kadhai*); add the lamb and fry till well browned. Add the ginger-garlic paste, turmeric powder, red chilli powder, garam masala and onion and tomato pastes. Reduce the heat and cook till the oil separates from the mixture.

3 Add the salt, sugar, yoghurt and 2½ cups water. Cook on low heat till the lamb is tender. Add the Bengal gram and bring the mixture to a boil. Lower the heat and simmer until well blended.

4 Serve hot, garnished with green coriander.

Dried, chopped, or powdered, adding small amounts of these **red chillies** to your food can provide your body with vitamin A and C, copper, and potassium.

SERVES 2–4

MANGSHO GHUGNI

Lamb with chickpeas

COOKING TIME
1 HOUR

• *Ingredients* •

- ½ cup / 100 g chickpeas (*kabuli chana*)
- 5 Tbsp / 75 ml vegetable oil
- ¼ cup / 42.5 g onions, chopped
- 1 tsp ginger paste
- 1 tsp garlic paste
- ¼ cup / 60 g tomato, chopped
- 200 g lamb, boneless pieces
- ½ tsp red chilli powder
- ½ tsp ground coriander (*dhaniya*)
- ½ tsp ground cumin (*jeera*)
- 1 cup / 240 ml water, plus more for soaking and boiling chickpeas
- Salt to taste
- 1 Tbsp / 1 g green coriander leaves (*hara dhaniya*), finely chopped

• *Method* •

1 Soak the chickpeas in water overnight. Drain and discard water. In a saucepan over medium heat, boil the chickpeas in 1½ cups water until soft. Without draining, set aside.

2 In a skillet over low-medium heat, heat the vegetable oil. Add the onions, ginger paste, garlic paste, tomato, and lamb. Mix well.

3 Add the red chilli powder, coriander, cumin, and 1 cup water. Season to taste with salt. Cook until the lamb is tender.

4 Add the boiled chickpeas along with the water in which they were boiled. Bring the mixture to a boil. Remove from the heat and serve hot, garnished with green coriander.

Adding **ginger** to your diet will reduce the risk of hypertension and high blood pressure, effectively helping you battle the risk of strokes and blood clots.

SERVES 6–8

KALA MASOOR DAL MA GOSHT

COOKING TIME
30–40 MINUTES

Lamb in a thick lentil gravy

• Ingredients •

- 1¼ cups / 250 g red gram (*masoor dal*), washed, soaked for 1 hour, drained
- 750 g lamb, cut into pieces
- 2 Tbsp / 30 ml vegetable oil
- 3–4 large onions, chopped lengthwise
- 2 Tbsp / 30 g ginger-garlic (*adrak-lasan*) paste
- 1½ tsp garam masala
- 1 tsp Parsi sambhar masala (available at grocery stores)
- 4 green chillies, whole
- ½ tsp turmeric (*haldi*) powder
- Salt to taste
- 3–4 medium-size tomatoes, finely chopped

• Method •

1 Heat the oil in a large pan; sauté the onions till golden brown. Add the ginger-garlic paste, garam masala, Parsi sambhar masala, green chillies, turmeric powder, and salt. Sauté for 5–10 minutes.

2 Add the tomatoes and cook on low heat till the water is completely absorbed.

3 Add the lamb and the drained gram; pressure-cook till 3 whistles or till done.

4 Take out a bowlful of gram from the cooker, mash well and put it back in the cooker. (This is done for a smooth gravy.)

5 Serve hot.

Green chillies have high quantities of antioxidant carotenoids, which have numerous health benefits. They have zero calories and can speed up one's metabolism after eating.

SERVES 4–6

SHAMMI KEBAB

Melt-in-the-mouth lamb patties

COOKING TIME
45 MINUTES

• Ingredients •

- 2 lb, 3 oz / 1 kg lamb, finely minced, without fat
- 1¼ cups / 250 g Bengal gram (*chana dal*), soaked for 30 minutes, drained
- 1 tsp cumin (*jeera*) seeds
- 1 1-in. piece ginger
- 1 medium-size onion, sliced, browned
- 1 Tbsp / 5 g coriander (*dhaniya*) seeds, powdered
- 2 tsp garam masala
- 2 eggs
- 4 green chillies, chopped
- 4 Tbsp / 4 g green coriander (*hara dhaniya*), chopped
- Salt to taste
- Vegetable oil for frying
- 1 medium-size onion, cut into rings
- 10 mint (*pudina*) leaves

• Method •

1 Add the lamb mince, drained Bengal gram, cumin seeds, ginger, and ½ cup water in a pressure cooker; cook till you hear the first whistle.

2 Turn off the heat, but do not open the cooker till the pressure dies down completely.

3 Now open the cooker, return to heat and cook till the mixture is completely dry. Remove and keep aside to cool.

4 When the mixture is cool enough to handle, add the browned onion and coriander powder. Grind the mixture on a stone slab or in a mixer.

5 Add the eggs, green chillies, green coriander, and salt. Mix well.

6 Divide the paste into 20 portions. Make small, round patties; slightly flatten them between your palms.

7 Refrigerate for 30 minutes before frying, to avoid the patties from breaking while frying.

8 Heat the oil in a wok (*kadhai*); deep-fry the patties, a few at a time, till brown. Remove with a slotted spoon and drain the excess oil on absorbent kitchen paper towels.

9 Serve hot, garnished with onion rings and mint leaves.

Mint is one of the most powerful medicinal herbs. With its anti-inflammatory properties, mint can provide relief to asthma patients by clearing congestion. It relieves headaches, eases nausea, and improves signs of depression.

DHANSAK

SERVES 6–8

Lamb cooked with mixed grams and vegetables

COOKING TIME
30 MINUTES

• Ingredients •

- ¼ cup / 50 g split red gram (*dhuli masoor dal*)
- 1 cup / 200 g pigeon peas (*toor dal*)
- ¼ cup / 50 g split green gram (*dhuli moong dal*)
- ¼ cup / 50 g split Bengal gram (*chana dal*)
- 3 Tbsp / 45 ml vegetable oil
- 3 medium-size onions, finely chopped
- 2 Tbsp / 30 g ginger-garlic (*adrak-lasan*) paste
- 2 Tbsp / 20 g dhansak masala (available at grocery stores)
- 2 lb, 3 oz / 1 kg lamb, cut into small pieces
- ¼ cup / 50 g red pumpkin (*lal kaddu*), chopped
- 1 small aubergine (*baigan*), chopped
- 2 small tomatoes, chopped
- 1 medium-size potato, chopped
- 3 cups / 720 ml water
- Salt to taste
- 1 tsp dried fenugreek leaves (*kasuri methi*)
- Fresh mint leaves, green coriander leaves, chopped green chillies, and lemon juice for garnishing

• Method •

1 In a large bowl, soak the split red gram, pigeon peas, split green gram, and split Bengal gram for 1 hour. Drain and set aside.

2 In a skillet over medium-high heat, heat the vegetable oil. Add the onions, ginger-garlic paste, and dhansak masala. Sauté until brown.

3 In a pressure cooker over medium heat, combine the meat, grams, pumpkin, aubergine, tomato, potato, the prepared onion mixture, and the water. Season to taste with salt.

4 Lock the lid in place and cook for 4–5 whistles, or until the meat is tender. Let the pressure release and remove the lid.

5 With a slotted spoon, transfer the meat pieces into a bowl. Mash and strain the remaining mixture. Cook for 6 minutes.

6 Add the cooked meat pieces to the mixture. Add the dried fenugreek leaves and simmer until it becomes thick like a broth.

7 Garnish with mint leaves, lemon juice, chopped green chillies, and green coriander. Best served with brown rice.

Dhansak Masala is made out of a combination of different spices, herbs, vegetables, and dals. It is a spice mix that has numerous health benefits for your cardiovascular, respiratory, renal and digestive health.

VEGETABLES

AND

FRUITS

SERVES 4–5

FADA NI KHICHRI

Green gram and broken wheat with vegetables

COOKING TIME
30 MINUTES

• *Ingredients* •

- 1 cup / 200 g split green gram (*dhuli moong dal*), washed, soaked for 15 minutes, drained
- ¾ cup / 160 g broken wheat (*dalia*), washed, soaked for 15 minutes, drained
- 1 cup / 160 g green peas (*hara matar*)
- 1 cup / 110 g potatoes, diced
- 1 cup / 100 g cauliflower florets
- 1 cup / 127 g onions, diced
- 1 Tbsp / 15 g green chilli-ginger paste
- ½ tsp black peppercorns (*sabut kali mirch*)
- 1 tsp red chilli powder
- ½ tsp turmeric (*haldi*) powder
- Salt to taste
- 2½ cups / 600 ml water, hot

For the tempering:

- 3 Tbsp / 45 g ghee
- 1 1-in. stick cinnamon (*dalchini*)
- 3 cloves (*laung*)
- 1 tsp cumin (*jeera*) seeds
- ¼ tsp asafoetida (*hing*)

• *Method* •

1 **For the tempering**, heat the ghee in a pressure cooker; add the cinnamon stick, cloves, cumin seeds, and asafoetida. Sauté for 30 seconds.

2 Add the green peas, potatoes, cauliflower, onions and the green chilli-ginger paste. Sauté for a few minutes, or till the vegetables are a little tender.

3 Add the drained split green gram and broken wheat, black peppercorns, red chilli powder, turmeric powder, and salt. Stir-fry for 4–5 minutes.

4 Add the hot water and pressure-cook for 3–4 whistles.

5 Allow the steam to escape, then open the pressure cooker carefully.

6 Stir vigorously, adding a little more hot water, if required, so that the split green gram and the broken wheat mix well. Adjust seasoning, if required.

7 Serve hot.

BEANS PORIYAL

SERVES 4–5

Beans with split black gram

COOKING TIME
20 MINUTES

• *Ingredients* •

- 2 lb, 3 oz / 1 kg beans (*sem*)
- ½ tsp turmeric (*haldi*) powder
- 1 tsp salt
- 4 Tbsp / 60 ml oil
- 1 tsp mustard seeds (*rai*)
- 1 tsp split black gram (*dhuli urad dal*)
- 2 red chillies, whole
- 2 medium-size onions, chopped
- 2 green chillies, chopped
- Salt to taste
- ½ coconut, fresh, grated

• *Method* •

1 Remove the strings from the beans and chop finely.

2 Boil the beans in 1 cup water, adding turmeric powder and salt. Cook until the beans are almost done. Drain excess water and keep aside.

3 Heat oil in a wok (*kadhai*). Add mustard seeds, split black gram and whole red chillies. When the mustard seeds begin to crackle, add chopped onions and green chillies.

4 Stir-fry for 4–5 minutes.

5 Add beans and stir-fry till beans are cooked.

6 Add salt to taste and the grated coconut; stir and remove from heat.

7 Serve immediately, accompanied by a curry dish and steamed rice or parathas.

SERVES 4

BHARWAN KARELAS

Stuffed bitter gourds

COOKING TIME
45 MINUTES

• Ingredients •

- 2 lb, 3 oz / 1 kg bitter gourds (*karela*)
- Mustard oil (*sarson ka tel*) for frying
- ¼ cup / 60 g ghee
- A pinch asafoetida (*hing*) powder
- ½ cup / 120 g yoghurt
- Salt to taste
- 1 tsp red chilli powder
- 1 tsp ginger paste
- ¼ cup / 60 g onion paste
- 2 tsp garlic paste
- 2 tsp ginger, chopped
- 2 tsp green chillies, chopped
- 1 tsp green coriander (*hara dhaniya*), chopped
- ½ cup / 120 ml water

For the filling:

- 2 tsp sugar
- 2 tsp salt
- ½ cup / 110 g potatoes, boiled, cut into ½-in. cubes
- ½ tsp cumin (*jeera*)
- ½ cup / 100 g Bengal gram (*chana dal*), boiled, drained
- 2 tsp tamarind (*imli*) pulp
- 2 tsp fennel (*saunf*)
- 1 tsp red chilli powder
- 3 Tbsp / 45 ml mustard oil (*sarson ka tel*)

• Method •

1 Scrape the bitter gourds and boil them in water till half cooked. Slit, remove seeds and squeeze them gently to remove water.

2 Heat mustard oil in a wok (*kadhai*); deep-fry the bitter gourds till crisp. Keep aside.

3 Heat ghee in a pan. Add asafoetida along with all the other ingredients except the water. Stir-fry for a few minutes, add water and cook till the water evaporates. Remove from heat.

4 Mix together ingredients for filling except mustard oil. Stuff the bitter gourds with the mixture and tie with a thread.

5 In a separate pan, heat 3 Tbsp mustard oil; add all the other ingredients along with the bitter gourds and cook till moisture evaporates. Remove and serve hot.

SERVES 8–10

SAI BHAJI

Bengal gram cooked with mixed vegetables

COOKING TIME
35 MINUTES

• Ingredients •

- 1 lb, 2 oz / 500 g spinach, washed, chopped
- 1 large onion, sliced
- 1 large potato, washed, cut into small pieces
- 2 carrots, washed, cut into rounds
- 6 French beans, washed, cut into small pieces
- ¼ cup / 50 g split Bengal gram (*chana dal*), soaked for 15 minutes
- ½ tsp turmeric (*haldi*) powder
- Salt to taste
- 1 1-in. piece ginger, finely chopped
- 3 green chillies, slit
- ½ Tbsp / 4 g wholewheat flour (*atta*)
- 1 tamarind (*imli*), soaked in water
- 2 Tbsp / 30 ml vegetable oil
- 6–8 garlic cloves, finely chopped
- 1 tsp red chilli powder

• Method •

1 Cook the vegetables with Bengal gram and turmeric powder in a pressure cooker till 2 whistles or 10 minutes. Let the steam come out. Then open the lid and mash the vegetables thoroughly.

2 Add salt, ginger, and green chillies; mix well.

3 Mix the flour in ¼ cup water Add tamarind pulp and add this mixture to the mashed vegetables and gram mixture.

4 Cook for a few minutes more without the lid.

5 Heat the oil in a small pan; fry the garlic till brown. Turn off the gas. Add red chilli powder and mix. Pour this into the vegetable mixture.

6 Serve hot.

Garlic acts as an antioxidant. With its anti-fungal and anti-bacterial properties, it can ward off infections.

SERVES 3–4

SURATI SALAD

Crunchy cucumber salad

COOKING TIME
5 MINUTES

• *Ingredients* •

- 1 tsp vegetable oil
- A pinch ground asafoetida (*hing*)
- 1 Tbsp / 12.5 g split Bengal gram (*chana dal*), roasted
- 1 Tbsp / 9 g peanuts, roasted, chopped
- 1 Tbsp / 4 g coconut, fresh, grated
- 1 tsp sesame seeds (*til*), roasted
- 2 green chillies, finely chopped
- ½ tsp sugar
- Salt to taste
- 1 cup / 300 g cucumber, small, diced

• *Method* •

1 In a skillet over medium-high heat, heat the vegetable oil.

2 Add the asafoetida and split Bengal gram. Sauté for 2 minutes.

3 In a large bowl, mix the peanuts, coconut, sesame seeds, green chillies, sugar, and salt.

4 Add the split Bengal gram-asafoetida mixture and cucumber. Taste to adjust the seasoning and serve.

Sesame seeds are oil-rich seeds. They are a good source of fiber, which supports digestive health and reduces obesity. The seeds are rich in protein, reduce inflammation, and support healthy bones.

VENGAYA SAMBHAR

SERVES 4–6

Onions in red gram gravy

COOKING TIME
20 MINUTES

• Ingredients •

- ¼ cup / 50 g red gram (*masoor dal*)
- ¼ tsp turmeric (*haldi*) powder
- Salt to taste
- 2 Tbsp / 30 ml refined oil
- ½ tsp mustard seeds (*rai*)
- 4–5 medium-size onions, diced into 6 pieces
- ¼ tsp fenugreek seeds (*methi dana*)
- 2–3 dried red chillies (*sookhi lal mirch*)
- A few curry leaves (*kadhi patta*)
- ½ tsp sambhar powder
- 1 lemon-size tamarind (*imli*), soaked in 2 cups / 480 ml of water for 20 minutes
- 1 green chilli, slit
- ¼ tsp asafoetida (*hing*)
- Green coriander (*hara dhaniya*) for garnishing

• Method •

1 Pressure-cook the red gram with turmeric powder and salt. Remove, mash lightly and keep aside.

2 Heat the oil in a wide-bottomed vessel; sauté the mustard seeds till they start crackling. Add onions and sauté for a while. Add fenugreek seeds, dried red chillies, and curry leaves; sauté for a minute. Take care to see that the onions do not burn.

3 Add sambhar powder; stir for a minute. Add tamarind extract, green chilli, and asafoetida; simmer on low heat until the onions are cooked.

4 Add the red gram and bring the mixture to a boil. Remove from heat. Serve garnished with green coriander and accompanied with steamed rice.

Red chillies have a number of beneficial effects on your cardiovascular system. They can reduce blood cholesterol and triglyceride levels, as well as prevent formation of blood clots.

SERVES 4

KATHRIKAI RASAVANGI

Aubergines in red gram gravy

COOKING TIME
20 MINUTES

• Ingredients •

- 2 cups / 166 g aubergines (*baigan*), quartered
- ½ cup / 100 g red gram (*masoor dal*)
- 1 Tbsp / 15 ml refined oil
- ¼ tsp mustard seeds (*rai*)
- Salt to taste
- A pinch turmeric (*haldi*) powder
- 1 lemon-size tamarind (*imli*), soaked
- in 2 cups / 480 ml water
- 1 tsp jaggery (*gur*) powder, optional
- A few curry leaves (*kadhi patta*)

For the paste:

- 1 Tbsp / 15 ml refined oil
- 2 Tbsp / 10 g coriander (*dhaniya*) seeds
- 2 Tbsp / 25 g Bengal gram (*chana dal*)
- A pinch asafoetida (*hing*)
- 1½ tsp black peppercorns (*sabut kali mirch*)

• Method •

1 Boil the red gram till cooked and keep aside.

2 **For the paste**, heat the oil; sauté all the ingredients for a minute. Remove and grind to a rough paste, sprinkling a little water if required. Keep aside.

3 Heat the oil; sauté the mustard seeds till they start crackling. Add the aubergines and sauté for 2 minutes till tender. Add salt, turmeric powder, and tamarind juice; cook on low heat till tender.

4 Add the cooked red gram and paste. Simmer for a minute till well blended. Add jaggery and mix well. Remove. Serve garnished with curry leaves.

Black peppercorns stimulate circulation and mucous flow in the body and can relive cold and cough. With their anti-bacterial properties, they can prevent the spread of infections.

SERVES 4

PAVAKAI PITLAY

Tangy bitter gourd and red gram

COOKING TIME
20 MINUTES

• Ingredients •

- 1 cup / 124 g bitter gourd (*karela*), medium-size, chopped into small pieces
- ½ cup / 100 g red gram (*masoor dal*)
- 1 lemon-size tamarind (*imli*), soaked
- in 2 cups / 480 ml warm water
- Salt to taste

For the paste:
- 1 Tbsp / 15 ml refined oil
- 2 Tbsp / 25 g Bengal gram (*chana dal*)
- 1 tsp black gram (*urad dal*)
- 1 Tbsp / 5 g coriander (*dhaniya*) seeds
- 1 dried red chilli (*sookhi lal mirch*)
- 1 Tbsp / 4 g coconut, grated

For the tempering:
- 1 Tbsp / 15 ml refined oil
- ½ tsp mustard seeds (*rai*)
- A few curry leaves (*kadhi patta*)

• Method •

1 Pressure-cook the red gram till done; keep aside.

2 For the paste, heat the oil; sauté all the ingredients except coconut. Remove and grind to a fine paste, adding coconut and a sprinkling of water.

3 Heat the tamarind juice; add salt and bitter gourd. Cook on low heat until soft. Add the paste and boiled red gram and continue to simmer for a couple of minutes till well blended.

4 For the tempering, crackle the mustard seeds and curry leaves in oil. Remove, add to the vegetable mixture and serve hot.

Mustard seeds are hot enough to break up congestion and stimulate appetite. They are an excellent source of vitamin A, calcium, potassium, and magnesium.

SERVES 4

VELLARIKAI KOSUMALLI

Cucumber medley

COOKING TIME
5 MINUTES

• Ingredients •

- ¼ cup / 50 g green gram (*moong dal*), soaked in warm water for 30 minutes, drained
- 1 medium-size cucumber, chopped into small cubes
- Salt to taste
- A pinch asafoetida (*hing*)
- 1 ½-in. piece ginger, finely chopped
- 1 green chilli, slit whole
- 1 Tbsp / 4 g coconut, grated
- Juice of 1 lemon
- A small bunch green coriander (*hara dhaniya*), finely chopped

• Method •

1 Mix all the ingredients together except the last two.

2 Serve sprinkled with lemon juice and garnished with green coriander.

Good for patients with diabetes, **coriander** stimulates insulin secretion in the body and lowers blood sugar levels. Coriander is great for the digestive system and supports bowel movements and liver function.

SERVES 2

ARAITHA SAMBHAR

Tangy pigeon peas cooked with vegetables

COOKING TIME
40 MINUTES

• Ingredients •

For the pigeon peas:

- ½ cup / 100 g pigeon peas (*toor dal*), soaked in water for 5 minutes, drained
- 2 cups / 480 ml water
- 4 Tbsp / 40 g Madras onion (pearl onion), chopped
- ½ tsp ground turmeric (*haldi*)
- Salt to taste
- ⅔ cup / 55 g aubergine (*baigan*), diced
- ½ medium-size green bell pepper, diced
- 1 long drumstick, diced
- 1 medium-size potato, diced
- 3 Tbsp / 30 g coconut, grated, dried, unsweetened
- 2 dried red chillies (*sookhi lal mirch*)
- 2½ tsp coriander (*dhaniya*) seeds
- ¾ tsp fenugreek seeds (*methi dana*)
- ½ tsp ground asafoetida (*hing*)
- 2 tsp split Bengal gram (*chana dal*)
- ¾ tsp cumin (*jeera*) seeds
- 2 tsp vegetable oil
- ½ tsp tamarind (*imli*) extract

For the tempering:

- 1 tsp vegetable oil
- ¾ tsp mustard seeds (*rai*)
- ½ tsp cumin (*jeera*) seeds
- ½ tsp aniseed (*saunf*)
- 2 dried red chillies (*sookhi lal mirch*)
- 3 curry leaves (*kadhi patta*)
- Salt to taste
- 2 Tbsp / 2 g green coriander leaves (*hara dhaniya*), finely chopped

• Method •

1 For the pigeon peas, in a saucepan over high heat, combine the pigeon peas and water and bring to a boil. Cook until tender.

2 Add the onion and turmeric. Season to taste with salt. Continue to cook until everything is soft. Remove the pot from the heat and set aside. Discard the water.

3 In a steamer basket, combine the aubergine, green bell pepper, drumstick, and potato. Steam until soft. Remove and set aside.

4 In a blender or mortar and pestle, grind the coconut, dried red chillies, coriander seeds, fenugreek seeds, asafoetida, split Bengal gram, cumin seeds, and vegetable oil into a smooth paste.

5 Add the steamed vegetables to the pigeon pea mix. Stir to combine, place the pan over low heat, and cook for 10–12 minutes.

6 Stir in the ground paste and tamarind extract. Cook for 5 minutes more.

7 For the tempering, in a wok over medium-high heat, heat the vegetable oil.

8 Add the mustard seeds, cumin seeds, aniseed, dried red chillies, and curry leaves. Sauté until the seeds begin to crackle and the curry leaves turn crisp. Pour the tempering into the pigeon peas and mix well. Season to taste with salt. Serve hot, garnished with coriander.

Fennel is used to support digestion and relieve issues like gas, heartburn, and bloating. It is a rich source of potassium, an essential component of our cells. This makes fennel a great natural way to regulate the body's blood pressure and heart rate.

BREADS

AND

CAKES

SERVES 6

KHAMAN DHOKLA

Steamed savoury cakes

COOKING TIME
20 MINUTES

• Ingredients •

- 1 cup / 200 g Bengal gram (*chana dal*), soaked overnight
- 4 green chillies
- 1 1-in. piece ginger
- 3 Tbsp / 45 ml vegetable oil
- Salt to taste
- ¼ tsp asafoetida (*hing*)
- ¼ tsp bicarbonate of soda

For the tempering:

- 1 Tbsp / 15 ml vegetable oil
- ½ tsp mustard seeds (*rai*)
- ½ tsp cumin (*jeera*) seeds
- 3–4 dried red chillies (*sookhi lal mirch*), whole
- 10 curry leaves (*kadhi patta*)
- ½ cup / 8 g green coriander (*hara dhaniya*), chopped
- ¼ coconut, grated

• Method •

1 Grind the green chillies and ginger to a smooth paste. Keep aside.

2 Grind the Bengal gram coarsely; whisk to incorporate air in it. Keep aside to ferment in a warm place for at least 10 hours or till tiny bubbles appear.

3 Add the oil, salt, asafoetida, bicarbonate of soda, and green chilli-ginger paste to the Bengal gram. Add a little water and whisk the mixture thoroughly once again.

4 Grease a flat stainless steel plate or a baking dish (2 in. deep). Spread the mixture to a thickness of 1 in. Steam till it is done. To check if the dish is ready, pierce with a fork. If the fork comes out clean, the *dhokla* is ready.

5 Allow to cool, then cut into 1–1½-in. squares.

6 **For the tempering**, heat the oil in a pan; add the mustard seeds, cumin seeds, and dried red chillies. When they start crackling, add the curry leaves and pour over the *dhokla*.

7 Serve garnished with coconut and green coriander.

SERVES 2–4

MOONG DAL KE CHILLE

Green gram pancakes

COOKING TIME
30 MINUTES

• Ingredients •

- 1¼ cups / 250 g green gram (*moong dal*), washed
- 2 Tbsp / 30 g ginger-garlic (*adrak-lasan*) paste
- 3 green chillies, chopped
- 1 Tbsp / 15 g green coriander (*hara dhaniya*), chopped
- Salt to taste
- Oil for frying

• Method •

1 Soak the green gram for 2–3 hours. Drain and grind to a fine paste, adding a little water.

2 Add the remaining ingredients, except oil, and mix well.

3 Add a little more water to bring the mixture to a dripping consistency.

4 Smear 2 tsp of oil in a non-stick pan; pour 2 Tbsp of the mixture in the pan and spread to form a flat round pancake. Cook over low heat till both the sides are golden brown in colour. Fry 6–8 such round pancakes.

5 Serve hot with chutney of your choice.

Coriander is used in many forms and is a good herb to boost your memory.

SERVES 12–13

MOONG DAL PURI

Stuffed green gram bread

COOKING TIME
30 MINUTES

• Ingredients •

- 2 cups / 250 g refined flour (*maida*)
- 3 Tbsp / 45 ml vegetable oil, plus more for roasting
- A pinch asafoetida (*hing*)
- ½ tsp cumin (*jeera*) seeds
- 1 cup / 200 g split green gram (*dhuli moong dal*), soaked for 2 hours, drained, ground to a paste
- 2 Tbsp / 16 g red chilli powder
- Salt to taste
- 1 tsp garam masala

• Method •

1 Heat 2 Tbsp oil in a pan; add asafoetida and cumin seeds, sauté for a few seconds. Add the green gram paste and the remaining ingredients, except oil and refined flour; sauté till the mixture is soft.

2 Rub 1 Tbsp oil into the refined flour and knead with enough water into a soft dough. Divide the dough equally into 12–13 portions.

3 Take a portion, make a hollow in the centre and fill with the green gram mixture. Seal the filling inside. Repeat with the other portions. Cover the stuffed balls with a moist cloth and keep aside for 10–15 minutes. Roll out each portion into a thin disc of 10-in. diameter with some dry flour.

4 Roast the disc on a griddle (*tawa*) on both sides with 1½ tsp oil. Remove and repeat with the other discs. Cover with aluminium foil. They can be eaten cold, if preferred.

URAD KACHORI

MAKES 20

Fried bread with black gram

COOKING TIME
30 MINUTES

• Ingredients •

- ½ cup / 100 g black gram (*urad dal*), soaked for 1½ hours
- 2 cups / 250 g refined flour (*maida*)
- 1 cup / 170 g semolina (*suji*)
- A pinch asafoetida (*hing*)
- ½ pinch onion seeds (*kalonji*)
- Salt to taste
- 1½ Tbsp / 22.5 ml vegetable oil

• Method •

1 Drain the black gram and grind to a smooth paste.

2 Mix the black gram paste with the remaining ingredients, except oil. Add a little water and knead to make a soft dough. Keep aside for 1 hour.

3 Before frying, knead the dough again with well-greased palms on a well-greased counter top. Divide the dough into lemon-size balls. Roll each ball out carefully into a 5-in. diameter disc.

4 Heat the oil in a wok (*kadhai*); fry the discs, one by one, turning them over frequently, on high heat till golden. They will be slightly white on the edges. Remove with a slotted spoon and drain the excess oil on paper towels. Serve hot.

Kalonji is very effective at lowering cholesterol levels in the body. It also has anti-bacterial properties which can fight off diseases.

SERVES 6

KALMI BARE

Fried mixed gram cakes

COOKING TIME
20 MINUTES

• Ingredients •

- 2 cups / 400 g Bengal gram (*chana dal*), washed, soaked for 4–5 hours, drained
- ½ cup / 100 g split black gram (*dhuli urad dal*), washed, soaked for 4–5 hours, drained
- 1 tsp salt
- 12 black peppercorns (*sabut kali mirch*), freshly ground
- 1 Tbsp / 15 g ginger, grated
- 2–3 green chillies, finely chopped
- A pinch asafoetida (*hing*)
- 1 Tbsp / 6 g cumin (*jeera*) seeds
- 2 Tbsp / 10 g coriander (*dhaniya*) seeds
- A bunch green coriander (*hara dhaniya*), finely chopped
- Ghee for frying

• Method •

1 Grind the Bengal gram and black gram separately to a coarse and grainy paste. Now mix the pastes and the remaining ingredients, except ghee.

2 With wet hands, take some paste and make a 3-in. wide, round cake. Repeat till all the mixture is used up.

3 Heat the ghee in a pan till hot; deep-fry the cakes, a few at a time. When small bubbles appear on the surface, turn and fry the other side till pale golden. Remove and drain the excess oil on absorbent kitchen towels. Keep aside to cool.

4 Then cut each cake into ¼-in. slices. Reheat the ghee and fry the slices till golden and crisp. Sprinkle some chaat masala, if desired, and serve with mint chutney.

Ginger can combat inflammation that can reduce pain and swelling in people with arthritis and can work against migraines.

SERVES 6–8

BHARVIN PURI

Black gram-stuffed fried bread

COOKING TIME
20 MINUTES

• *Ingredients* •

- 5 cups / 625 g wholewheat flour (*atta*)
- Salt to taste
- 2 Tbsp / 30 ml vegetable oil

For the stuffing:

- 1 cup / 200 g whole black gram (*sabut urad dal*), soaked overnight, drained
- A pinch asafoetida (*hing*)
- 1 Tbsp / 6 g fennel (*saunf*), pounded
- 4 tsp coriander (*dhaniya*) seeds, crushed
- 1 tsp red chilli powder
- Vegetable oil for frying

• *Method* •

1 Sift the flour and salt. Mix in the oil and knead with enough water to make a smooth dough.

2 **For the stuffing**, remove the skin of the black gram by rubbing between your palms. Grind the black gram with all the spices to a coarse, sticky paste.

3 Divide the flour dough equally into 20 balls. Flatten each ball, grease the top surface and add 1 Tbsp paste. Bring the edges together to seal the filling. Make a ball and roll each out to a 3-in. disc. Repeat with the other balls.

4 Heat the oil in a wok (*kadhai*); deep-fry the discs, on low heat, till golden on both sides. Remove and drain. Before serving, fry the puffs again till crisp.

5 Serve hot.

Fennel is a natural diuretic. It removes toxins and reduces the risk of urinary tract infections. It can also reduce asthmatic symptoms and can aid with nasal congestion and cough.

MAKES 10

ADAI

Mixed gram pancakes

COOKING TIME
45 MINUTES

• Ingredients •

- 2½ cups / 500 g rice, parboiled
- ½ cup / 100 g Bengal gram (*chana dal*)
- ½ cup / 100 g black gram (*urad dal*)
- ½ cup / 100 g red gram (*masoor dal*)
- 3–4 dried red chillies (*sookhi lal mirch*)
- ½ coconut, grated, optional
- Salt to taste
- ¼ tsp asafoetida (*hing*)
- A small bunch drumstick leaves, chopped, optional
- 6–7 Tbsp / 90–105 ml refined oil

• Method •

1 Soak the rice, all the grams, and dried red chillies in 2 cups water.

2 Drain and grind roughly in a grinder, adding a sprinkling of water if necessary. Add the coconut, salt, asafoetida, and drumstick leaves (optional).

3 Pour 2 ladlefuls of batter onto a wide, greased pan and spread out thick. Pour a little oil in the centre and around the edges. Cook till golden brown. Turn the other side and cook till golden brown. Remove and repeat till all the batter is used up.

4 Serve hot with coconut chutney and powdered jaggery, if desired.

Asafoetida is a natural blood thinner, it can lower blood pressure levels and alleviate menstrual cramps for women by helping the blood flow smoothly through the body.

SERVES 2

DAR NI PORI

Stuffed wheat and rice cake

COOKING TIME
25–30 MINUTES

• Ingredients •

For the rice crust:
- ½ cup / 80 g rice flour
- ½ cup / 120 g ghee
- A pinch salt

For the wheat flour rounds:
- ½ cup / 85 g semolina (*suji*)
- 5 Tbsp / 40 g wholewheat flour (*atta*)
- A pinch salt
- ½ cup / 120 ml water
- 1 tsp rose water
- 1 tsp ghee

For the stuffing:
- 1½ cups / 300 g split red gram (*dhuli masoor dal*), washed, drained
- 1½ cups / 300 g sugar
- 2 tsp nutmeg-cardamom (*jaiphal-elaichi*) powder
- 1 tsp vanilla essence
- 4 Tbsp / 60 g ghee
- ½ tsp black cumin (*shahi jeera*) seeds, ground
- 1 Tbsp / 15 g raisins (*kishmish*)
- 1½ Tbsp / 15 g crystallized cherries, finely chopped
- 1 Tbsp / 10 g onion seeds (*kalonji*)

• Method •

1 **For the rice crust**, put the ghee in a large, round container and whip with your palm till it liquefies.

2 Gradually add the rice flour and salt and knead with your palms into a smooth dough.

3 Divide the dough equally into 2 rounds and place them in a bowl of ice-cold water.

4 **For the wheat flour rounds**, combine the semolina, wholewheat flour and salt in a large bowl.

5 Add the water and knead into a soft dough.

6 Add the rose water and ghee, and knead for 10 more minutes. Divide equally into 2 rounds; keep aside.

7 **For the stuffing**, cook the split red gram in a pressure cooker with 2½ cups water for about 15 minutes until soft. Transfer into a large vessel and add the sugar, nutmeg-cardamom powder, vanilla essence, 2 Tbsp ghee, and black cumin seeds. Mix well.

8 Add the raisins, cherries, and onion seeds, and if the red gram is not thick, reheat and cool till it thickens.

9 Spread one of the wholewheat flour rounds onto a flat surface with your fingertips till it becomes circular and is the size of a quarter plate. Then take one ball of the rice crust which was put in water and spread it over the wholewheat flour layer, making it into a flat circle roughly 5–6 in. in diameter. Similarly, make a disc of the second rice flour crust and wholewheat flour round.

10 Divide the red gram mixture into 2 equal portions and place each on the two flattened layers. Fold the layer over the gram and roll into a ball. Pat the stuffed roll flat with your palm till it is 6 in. wide. Repeat with the second round.

11 Heat 1 Tbsp ghee on an iron griddle (*tawa*); place one stuffed round carefully in the centre. Cook for 5 minutes on each side, shifting it back and forth with 2 pieces of soft cloth till golden brown. Repeat with the second round.

12 Cut into wedges and serve hot with tea.

Nutmegs contain compounds that aid digestion. They can resolve diarrhea, constipation, gas and bloating. Nutmegs are also believed to be able to stimulate the nerves in the brain. They are effective in treating anxiety, depression and have been shown to induce sleep.

SIDES

AND

ACCOMPANIMENTS

SERVES 6–8

MAG NI DAL NA BHAJIYA

Fried green gram dumplings

COOKING TIME
30 MINUTES

• Ingredients •

- 1 lb, 2 oz / 500 g split green gram (*dhuli moong dal*), with skin, soaked for 4 hours or overnight
- 4 green chillies
- 15 black peppercorns (*sabut kali mirch*), coarsely ground
- A pinch asafoetida (*hing*)
- Salt to taste
- Vegetable oil for deep frying

• Method •

1 Remove the skin of the green gram by rubbing between your palms and then washing in plenty of water. Drain the excess water.

2 Add the green chillies, pepper and asafoetida and blend to a smooth paste without adding any water.

3 Transfer the mixture into a large bowl and then whisk well with your hand, till light and fluffy.

4 Heat the oil in a wok (*kadhai*); gently drop spoonfuls of the mixture and deep-fry on medium heat for about 3 minutes or until golden brown and crisp. Remove and drain the excess oil. Repeat till all the batter is used up.

5 Serve hot with chutney of your choice.

Black peppercorns are a nourishing spice which provides respiratory relief from cold and coughs. It possesses anti-bacterial, antioxidant, and immune-boosting properties.

SERVES 2–4

FANGEVELA MAG

Sprouted green gram salad

COOKING TIME
10 MINUTES

• Ingredients •

- 1⅔ cups / 333 g whole green gram (*sabut moong dal*), soaked for 8 hours
- 1 tsp vegetable oil
- ½ tsp mustard seeds (*rai*)
- ¼ tsp asafoetida (*hing*)
- 1½ cups / 360 ml water
- ¼ tsp bicarbonate of soda
- Salt to taste
- ½ tsp sugar
- 1 tsp cumin (*jeera*) powder
- ¼ tsp turmeric (*haldi*) powder
- ¾ tsp red chilli powder
- 1 tsp coriander (*dhaniya*) powder

• Method •

1 Drain the green gram and tie in a muslin cloth. Keep the cloth inside a vessel in a cool place and cover it tightly. Keep aside for 24 hours to allow the green gram to sprout.

2 Heat the oil in a pan; add the mustard seeds. Once they crackle, add the asafoetida and the sprouted green gram.

3 Add the water, bicarbonate of soda, salt, sugar, and the spices. Mix well. Cook covered for 10 minutes or until tender.

4 Serve hot, with any *kadhi* (thick gravy based on chickpea flour), if preferred.

Cumin is a good source of iron and has plant compounds which function as antioxidants. It can improve the health of your skin, fight infections, and prevent diabetes.

MOONG DAL SHEERA

SERVES 4

A traditional sweet made of green gram

COOKING TIME
30 MINUTES

• Ingredients •

- 1 cup / 200 g split green gram (*dhuli moong dal*), soaked for 5 hours
- 6 Tbsp / 90 g ghee
- 1 cup / 240 ml milk, hot
- 1 cup / 240 ml water, warm
- 1 cup / 200 g sugar
- A few strands saffron (*kesar*), dissolved in 1 Tbsp / 15 ml hot milk
- 5 green cardamom (*choti elaichi*) seeds, powdered
- 10 almonds, blanched, cut into slivers
- 10 pistachios, blanched, cut into slivers

• Method •

1 Drain the split green gram and grind to a coarse paste, using very little water. Drain the excess water that may remain after the grinding is over.

2 Heat the ghee in a wok (*kadhai*); add the split green gram paste and stir continuously on low heat till it becomes golden brown.

3 Add the milk and warm water; cook, stirring continuously, till the mixture is absolutely dry.

4 Add the sugar and cook on low heat till the oil separates. Add the saffron and green cardamom powder; mix well.

5 Serve hot, garnished with almonds and pistachios.

Saffron helps with inflammation, reduces appetite and aids in weight loss. It reduces the risk of cardiovascular diseases.

CRISPY BENGAL GRAM STRIPS

SERVES 4–6

COOKING TIME
30 MINUTES

• Ingredients •

- 1 cup / 200 g Bengal gram (*chana dal*)
- 3 Tbsp / 15 g coriander (*dhaniya*) seeds
- 1 Tbsp / 15 g black peppercorns (*sabut kali mirch*)
- 2 tsp ginger, chopped
- 1 cup / 16 g green coriander (*hara dhaniya*), chopped
- 2 green chillies, chopped
- Salt to taste
- 1 tsp red chilli powder
- 1 tsp garam masala
- Oil for frying

• Method •

1 Soak Bengal gram for 4–5 hours or in warm water for 30 minutes. Drain and blend along with coriander seeds and peppercorns to make a coarsely ground, thick paste.

2 Put the paste into a big bowl with the remaining ingredients except the oil. Mix thoroughly, keep for 30 minutes.

3 Heat oil in a wok (*kadhai*) till it starts smoking. Moisten hands and shape the mixture into 10-cm flat patties. Fry patties for 2–3 minutes on both sides and remove from oil. Drain excess oil and allow to cool.

4 Slice the patties into 3–4 strips. Reheat oil till it starts smoking. Lower heat to medium and fry the strips till they are crisp and golden brown on both sides. Drain excess oil and serve hot.

SERVES 6–8

MOGAR

Dry and spicy green gram

COOKING TIME
20 MINUTES

• Ingredients •

- 1¼ cups / 250 g split green gram (*dhuli moong dal*), soaked for 30 minutes, drained
- 4 Tbsp / 60 g ghee
- ½ tsp cumin (*jeera*) seeds
- A pinch asafoetida (*hing*)
- 1–2 bay leaves (*tej patta*)
- ½ tsp turmeric (*haldi*) powder
- 1 tsp red chilli powder
- 1 tsp salt
- 2 tsp coriander (*dhaniya*) powder
- ½ tsp garam masala
- 1 tsp mango powder (*amchoor*)
- ½ tsp sugar

• Method •

1 Heat the ghee in a wok (*kadhai*); add the cumin seeds, asafoetida, and bay leaves. When they start spluttering, add the turmeric powder and red chilli powder; sauté for a few minutes. Add ½ cup water, mix well.

2 Add the drained green gram, salt, coriander powder, and 1 cup water, stir occasionally, and cook till the mixture is completely dry.

3 Before removing from heat, add garam masala, mango powder, and sugar. Mix lightly and serve.

Bay leaves are packed with vitamins A, C, magnesium, calcium, potassium, iron and manganese. They have antimicrobial, anti-fungal and anti-bacterial properties which support the body's immune system.

SERVES 5–6

DAHI PAKORI

Fried pulse dumplings in yoghurt

COOKING TIME
20 MINUTES

• Ingredients •

For the pakoris:

- ½ cup / 100 g split green gram (*dhuli moong dal*)
- ½ cup / 100 g black gram (*urad dal*)
- 1 1-in. piece ginger, grated
- A pinch bicarbonate of soda
- Salt to taste
- Vegetable oil for frying
- 2½ cups / 600 g yoghurt, strained
- 1 tsp red chilli powder
- 1 tsp cumin (*jeera*) seeds, roasted, powdered
- ½ cup / 120 g tamarind chutney
- 2 Tbsp / 30 g green coriander relish

• Method •

1 **For the pakoris**, after soaking the green and black gram for 2 hours, grind to a smooth paste. Add ginger, bicarbonate of soda and salt. Whip till the batter is smooth, and of dropping consistency.

2 Heat the oil in a pan; carefully drop tablespoons of the batter into the hot oil. Fry till golden brown. Remove with a slotted spoon and immerse the dumplings in salted water for 5–7 minutes. Repeat till all the batter is used up.

3 Remove the soaked dumplings; squeeze out the excess water and arrange them in a bowl.

4 Mix salt with the yoghurt and pour over the dumplings. Sprinkle the spices, tamarind and green coriander relish; serve.

Tamarind can maintain a healthy blood pressure and wash out the toxins in your kidneys. The substantial qualities of vitamin C can improve the immune system.

PUNJABI CHANA

SERVES 4–6

Chickpeas with spices

COOKING TIME
1 HOUR

• Ingredients •

- 1½ cups / 300 g chickpeas (*kabuli chana*), soaked in water for 2 hours, drained
- ½ tsp baking powder
- Salt to taste
- ½ cup / 120 g ghee
- 6 tsp garlic paste
- 10 red chillies, ground with a little water
- 6 tsp coriander seeds (*sabut dhaniya*), ground with a little water
- 3 cups / 720 g tomatoes, chopped
- 10 green chillies, slit
- 1⅓ Tbsp / 20 g ginger, finely chopped
- 3 Tbsp / 45 ml lemon juice
- 2 tsp garam masala

• Method •

1 Boil the chickpeas in sufficient water with baking powder and salt until tender. Drain them and keep aside.

2 Heat the ghee in a pan; add the garlic paste and fry until golden. Add the red chillies and coriander seed pastes. Stir-fry until the water evaporates.

3 Add the tomatoes, green chillies and ¾ of the ginger. Bring to a boil, reduce the heat and cook until the ghee comes to the surface.

4 Add the boiled chickpeas to the mixture. Cook for 5 minutes. Add the lemon juice and garam masala. Stir well.

5 Serve hot, garnished with the remaining ginger.

The spices used in **Garam Masala** have anti-inflammatory and antioxidant properties which can improve digestion, reduce inflammation and boost your metabolism and immunity.

SERVES 2–4

SOOKHI URAD DAL

Dry black gram with aromatic spices

COOKING TIME
45 MINUTES

• Ingredients •

- 1 cup / 200 g split black gram (*dhuli urad dal*), washed, drained
- 1 tsp turmeric (*haldi*) powder
- Salt to taste
- ½ cup / 120 g ghee
- ½ cup / 85 g onions, chopped
- 3 tsp garlic, finely chopped
- 4 tsp ginger, thinly sliced
- 6 green chillies, finely chopped
- 1 tsp cumin (*jeera*) seeds
- 1 tsp red chilli powder
- ¼ tsp asafoetida (*hing*)
- 2 medium-size tomatoes, chopped
- ½ cup / 8 g green coriander (*hara dhaniya*), chopped

• Method •

1 Boil the split black gram in 2 cups water with turmeric powder and salt. Cook until it turns soft and a little water remains.

2 Heat the ghee in a wok (*kadhai*); add the onions, garlic and ginger and sauté till light brown. Add the green chillies, cumin seeds, red chilli powder, asafoetida, tomatoes and green coriander.

3 Cook for a few minutes till the tomatoes turn soft. Then add this mixture to the cooked split black gram and mix well.

4 Serve hot.

Garlic has antibacterial effects on the bacteria that causes dental plaque. It can treat oral infections and can prevent tooth decay. It can also help against skin rashes and allergies.

SERVES 6–8

DAL JI KACHORI

Deep-fried green gram fritters

COOKING TIME
20 MINUTES

• *Ingredients* •

- 1½ cups / 300 g split green gram (*dhuli moong dal*), with husk, soaked overnight, washed the next morning, husk removed
- 3 green chillies, finely chopped
- 1 tsp dried red chillies (*sookhi lal mirch*), coarsely ground
- 1 1-in. piece ginger, finely chopped
- 4 Tbsp / 4 g green coriander (*hara dhaniya*), finely chopped
- Salt to taste
- Vegetable oil for frying

• *Method* •

1 Grind the gram coarsely in a blender. Beat it with a spoon till frothy.

2 Add all the ingredients except oil.

3 Heat the oil in a wok (*kadhai*); with a medium-size spoon, pour the gram mixture into the hot oil, a few spoons at a time, and fry till brown. Remove with a slotted spoon and drain the excess oil on absorbent kitchen towels. Repeat till all the batter is used up.

4 These fritters can be reheated before serving.

5 Serve with green chutney.

SERVES 8

KHASTA KACHORI

Deep-fried flour puffs

COOKING TIME
10 MINUTES

• Ingredients •

- 2 cups / 250 g refined flour (*maida*)
- Salt to taste
- A pinch bicarbonate of soda
- 1 Tbsp / 15 g ghee, plus more for frying

For the filling:

- 1 cup / 200 g split black gram (*dhuli urad dal*), washed,
- soaked for 2 hours, drained
- 1 tsp cumin (*jeera*) seeds
- A pinch asafoetida (*hing*)
- 2 tsp coriander (*dhaniya*) powder
- ½ tsp red chilli powder
- 1 tsp salt
- Vegetable oil for frying

• Method •

1 Sift the flour, salt, and bicarbonate of soda. Rub in the ghee and knead with enough water to make a hard dough. Keep aside for 30 minutes.

2 **For the filling**, grind all the ingredients except the oil together coarsely on a stone slab or in a mixer. Sauté the filling in 1 Tbsp ghee till golden. Keep aside to cool.

3 Divide the flour dough into 16 balls. Shape each ball into a small cup; fill 1 Tbsp filling into the hollow, pinch together to seal and pat into rounds.

4 Heat the oil in a wok (*kadhai*); deep-fry the rounds, a few at a time, on low heat till they puff up and become crisp and golden. Remove and drain the excess oil on absorbent kitchen towels.

5 Serve hot.

SERVES 4

SOOKHE KABULI CHANE

COOKING TIME
1 HOUR

Spicy chickpeas cooked dry

• Ingredients •

- 1½ cups / 300 g chickpeas (*kabuli chana*)
- 1 tsp bicarbonate of soda
- 1 tea bag
- 2 Tbsp / 10 g coriander (*dhaniya*) seeds
- 1 Tbsp / 6 g cumin (*jeera*) seeds
- 1 tsp red chilli powder
- 2 tsp pomegranate seeds, ground
- ¼ Tbsp / 7.5 g dried mango powder (*amchoor*)
- 2 tsp garam masala
- Salt to taste
- 2 medium-size potatoes, cut into fingers, fried
- 1 2-in. piece ginger, julienned, fried
- ½ cup / 120 ml vegetable oil
- 2 green chillies
- 1 dried red chilli (*sookhi lal mirch*), chopped
- 1 medium-size onion, cut into rings

• Method •

1 Soak the chickpeas overnight with bicarbonate of soda. Next morning, boil the chickpeas with the tea bag in plenty of water, on low heat, till they are tender and the water nearly dries up. Discard the tea bag.

2 Add all the dry spices, salt, fried potato fingers, and ginger; toss well.

3 Heat the oil in a pan; add the chickpea mixture, and toss on low heat for about 10 minutes.

4 Serve hot, garnished with green chillies, dried red chilli, and onions rings.

Adding **cumin seeds** would help you employ their cardiovascular benefits like reducing high blood pressure and protection against myocardial injuries. They also have a positive effect on your nervous system and can improve your memory.

SERVES 3–4

SOOKHI DAL

Black gram cooked dry

COOKING TIME
10 MINUTES

• Ingredients •

- 1 cup / 200 g split black gram (*dhuli urad dal*), soaked overnight
- 1 Tbsp / 15 g ghee
- 1 tsp cumin (*jeera*) seeds
- 4 green chillies, slit
- 1 medium-size onion, sliced, fried
- ¼ tsp garam masala
- 1 tsp dried mango powder (*amchoor*)
- ½ tsp black pepper
- Salt to taste

• Method •

1 Rub the split black gram with your hands to remove the skin. Drain.

2 Heat the ghee in a pan; add the cumin seeds and green chillies. When they start spluttering, add the black gram and salt; stir-fry for 4–5 minutes.

3 Pour 2 cups water; cook on high heat till a little water remains. Lower the heat and simmer till the grains are cooked and the mixture is dry. Stir gently and occasionally so that the grains don't break and stick to the bottom of the pan.

4 Transfer to a bowl; garnish with fried onion, garam masala, mango powder, and black pepper. A dollop of butter or hot ghee can be added to enhance the flavour.

MAKES 12–15

THAIR VADAIS

Spicy dahi vadas

COOKING TIME
1 HOUR

• Ingredients •

For the vadai (dumplings):

- 2 cups / 400 g split black gram (*dhuli urad dal*), soaked in water overnight, drained
- Salt to taste
- ½ cup / 32 g curry leaves (*kadhi patta*), chopped
- 2 green chillies, finely chopped
- 1 Tbsp / 15 g ginger, crushed, peeled, fresh
- 1 Tbsp / 15 ml lemon juice, freshly squeezed
- ½ tsp ground asafoetida (*hing*) stirred into ½ cup / 120 ml water

For spice mix:

- 2 dried red chillies (*sookhi lal mirch*)
- 1 tsp cumin (*jeera*) seeds
- ½ tsp black mustard seeds (*rai*)

For the yoghurt:

- 2 tsp vegetable oil
- ½ cup / 32 g curry leaves (*kadhi patta*), chopped
- 4 green chillies
- 3 cups / 720 g yoghurt
- 1 cup / 240 ml water
- Salt to taste
- Vegetable oil for deep-frying

• Method •

1 For the *vadai*, in a blender or food processor, grind the split black gram to a paste. Add salt, the curry leaves, green chillies, ginger, lemon juice, and asafoetida water. Blend into a stiff batter and set aside.

2 For the spice mix, in a blender or mortar and pestle, coarsely crush the dried red chillies, cumin seeds, and mustard seeds.

3 For the yoghurt, in a wok over low-medium heat, heat the vegetable oil. Add the spice mix, curry leaves, and green chillies. Cook for a few seconds. Stir in the yoghurt and water. Season to taste with salt. Transfer to a bowl and set aside.

4 To finish the *vadai*, clean the wok and return it to the heat. Heat the vegetable oil. Have a bowl of cold water nearby. Gently lower spoonfuls of the black gram batter into the hot oil and deep-fry the *vadais* until golden. Remove and drain on paper towels. Transfer the *vadais* to the water for a few seconds. Remove and gently squeeze out the excess water. Repeat with the remaining batter. Add the *vadais* to the spiced yoghurt and serve cold.

MAKES 10

AMAVADAI

Deep-fried mixed gram rounds

COOKING TIME
15 MINUTES

• Ingredients •

- ½ cup / 100 g Bengal gram (*chana dal*)
- ¾ cup / 150 g black gram (*urad dal*)
- ½ cup / 100 g red gram (*masoor dal*)
- 2 dried red chillies (*sookhi lal mirch*)
- Salt to taste
- A pinch asafoetida (*hing*)
- 2 cups / 480 ml refined oil

• Method •

1 Soak the grams in enough water to cover for an hour. Drain excess water and grind with dried red chillies, salt, and asafoetida to a coarse batter.

2 Heat the oil in a pan. Roll the *vadai* mixture into balls and flatten on the palm into thick, small rounds (or on a piece of banana leaf, keeping the leaf on your left palm, flatten out the paste with the tips of your right-hand finger). Do not make a hole in the centre of the *vadai*.

3 Lower the rounds into the hot oil and fry till golden. Remove with a slotted spoon and drain the excess oil on absorbent kitchen towels. Repeat till all the rounds are fried.

SERVES 4

PARUPPU THUVAIYAL

Red gram chutney

COOKING TIME
2 MINUTES

• Ingredients •

- ½ cup / 100 g red gram (*masoor dal*)
- 1 Tbsp / 15 ml refined oil
- 2 dried red chillies (*sookhi lal mirch*)
- ¼ tsp asafoetida (*hing*)
- Salt to taste

• Method •

1 Heat the oil in a pan; add the red gram and dried red chillies and sauté till the gram turns golden. Add the remaining ingredients and sauté for 2 minutes. Remove and keep aside to cool.

2 When cool, grind to a paste in a grinder, adding a little water.

3 Serve with rice.

Asafoetida is known to assist pancreatic cells in secreting insulin and maintaining blood sugar levels. It can stimulate the nerves in the body and can be used with many types of nerve disorders.

SERVES 4

DANGUR PACHADI

Powdered black gram in yoghurt

COOKING TIME
5 MINUTES

• Ingredients •

- ¼ cup / 50 g black gram (*urad dal*)
- 1 cup / 240 g yoghurt, made thin with ¼ cup / 60 ml water
- 1 Tbsp / 15 ml refined oil
- 1 tsp mustard seeds (*rai*)
- 1 green chilli, slit whole
- ½ tsp cumin (*jeera*) seeds
- Salt to taste
- A pinch asafoetida (*hing*)

• Method •

1 Heat ½ Tbsp oil in a pan; sauté the black gram for a while. Remove and powder in a grinder.

2 Heat the remaining oil in a pan; sauté the mustard seeds till they start crackling; add green chilli and cumin seeds; sauté for a while. Remove from heat quickly.

3 Mix the powdered black gram with the yoghurt. Add salt and asafoetida; mix well.

4 Add the mustard seed mixture and mix well.

Mustard comes from a strong anticancer group of plants and is strong enough to provide protection against uterine cancer. With their anti-fungal and anti-bacterial properties, these seeds can prevent and fight infections.

SERVES 4

VAZHAPOO PARUPPUSHILI

Banana flower and red gram crumble

COOKING TIME
50 MINUTES

• Ingredients •

- 1 banana flower (*kele ka phool*), whole
- 4 Tbsp / 60 ml refined oil
- ½ tsp mustard seeds (*rai*)
- Salt to taste
- 2 dried red chillies (*sookhi lal mirch*)
- A pinch asafoetida (*hing*)

For the paste:

- ½ cup / 100 g red gram (*masoor dal*), soaked for 1 hour, drained

• Method •

1 **For the paste**, grind all the ingredients together in a grinder to a coarse paste.

2 Place this mixture in a steamer and steam for 30–40 minutes or until soft. Keep aside.

3 Smear some oil on the fingertips and remove the inner edible part of the flower and a short part of the stem and chop into pieces. Keep aside in a bowl of water (to prevent it from turning black).

4 Heat 2 Tbsp oil in a pan; sauté the mustard seeds till they start crackling. Drain the banana flower, add to the pan and sauté for 2 minutes.

5 Add the red gram paste; sauté for another 2 minutes on low heat until well blended. Serve hot.

MOONG SABUT

SERVES 4–6

Whole green gram

COOKING TIME
20 MINUTES

• Ingredients •

- 1 cup / 200 g whole green gram (*sabut moong dal*), soaked for 1 hour
- 1 Tbsp / 15 ml vegetable oil
- 1 tsp cumin (*jeera*) seeds
- ½ tsp turmeric (*haldi*) powder
- ½ tsp salt
- 1 tsp red chilli powder
- ½ tsp raw mango powder (*amchoor*)

• Method •

1 Heat the oil in a pressure cooker; add cumin seeds. When the seeds begin to crackle, add green gram and turmeric powder; mix well.

2 Add just enough water to cover the gram and cook on low heat till 2 whistles.

3 Take the steam out so that gram is not overcooked.

4 Transfer the gram into a serving dish. Sprinkle with salt, red chilli powder, and mango powder.

5 Stir with a fork. The gram grains should be separate and dry.

6 This is an ideal side dish, often served as a light breakfast.

Aamchoor is rich in iron and is very nutritious for pregnant women. Eating it regularly can improve your eyesight and prevents related diseases like cataract. It can clear acne and blackheads and can detoxify your skin.